Community Planning and Conceptions of Change

COMMUNITY PLANNING AND CONCEPTIONS OF CHANGE

Peter Marris

Routledge & Kegan Paul
London, Boston, Melbourne and Henley

First published in 1982
by Routledge & Kegan Paul Ltd
39 Store Street, London WC1E 7DD,
9 Park Street, Boston, Mass. 02108, USA,
296 Beaconsfield Parade, Middle Park,
Melbourne, 3206, Australia and
Broadway House, Newtown Road,
Henley-on-Thames, Oxon RG9 1EN
Printed in Great Britain by
Billing & Sons, Worcester

Library of Congress Cataloging in Publication Data
Marris, Peter.
Community planning and conceptions of change.
Bibliography: p.
Includes index.
1. Urban renewal. 2. Community development,
Urban. 3. Land use, Urban. 4. Social action,
5. Urban economics. I. Title.
HT170.M33 1982 307'.12 82-13175
ISBN 0-7100-9349-7

CONTENTS

ACKNOWLEDGMENTS

The research for, and writing of this book was supported by a grant from the Ford Foundation. I would like to thank, especially, Francis X. Sutton of the Foundation, for his encouragement and good advice over twenty-five years, as our interests and work converged so often on the same topics of mutual concern. I owe him a great deal.

I began the research for this book at the Centre for Environmental Studies, and the support and critical advice of David Donnison, who was then the Centre's Director, was of the greatest help. Later, when I was completing the book in America, Robert Kraushaar acted as my research assistant in Britain gathering much important information and reviewing my drafts. John Benington, Cynthia Cockburn, Marjorie Mayo, S. Michael Miller, Robert S. Weiss and Peter Willmott also read all or part of the book in draft and made very helpful comments. I would like, also, to thank Etsuko Otomo, Kitty Bednar, and Marsha Brown for typing the manuscript.

Throughout the whole endeavour, Dolores Hayden was my constant intellectual companion, helping me to clarify and develop my thoughts, commenting on drafts, and suggesting new perspectives, generously giving time from the pressing demands of her own scholarly work.

1 INTRODUCTION

In most of the older industrial cities of Britain and America,
just beyond the new civic centre, the municipal parking structures and the glazed towers of corporate offices, lies an area of
desolation. Whole blocks have been razed, leaving a wasteland of
rubble and scrap, through which willow herbs and grasses poke
their stems. Some buildings may be gutted by fire or boarded up.
Here and there, sometimes, a new housing project stands bleakly
on its rubbish-strewn platform of concrete, disfigured by graffiti and broken glass, waiting for a context of human activity to
redeem its barrenness. The whole neighbourhood looks, as it is,
abandoned - by landlords, by city government, by urban redevelopment, by industry and commerce: the victim of haphazard
and unfinished projects in which the originators have long since
lost interest. Millions of British and American families live in
neighbourhoods like this, partly because their friends are here,
but mostly because they have nowhere else to go.

Ever since they were first built over as workers' tenements and
cottages, these inner city neighbourhoods have concentrated the
cruelties and tensions of industrial capitalism, setting the stage on
which exploitation, charity, class struggle and reform appeared
most vividly and most in character. Here in the nineteenth century housing reformers came to put down plague and moral deg-
radation, municipal reformers to put down political corruption,
charitable workers to uplift poverty and social investigators to
describe its indomitable reality. In these streets great strikes
were organized and doggedly sustained. So, too, the recent history of social policy and social protest, in Britain and America,
turns largely on the problems these inner city neighbourhoods
present - from slum clearance and urban renewal, new towns and
model cities, to anti-poverty programmes, community action,
Black Power, welfare rights, rent strikes and tenants' movements.
Here in the inner city the social costs of industrial capitalism have
been laid out most obviously, and often most threateningly, for all
to see. How people understood what they saw and responded to
it has crystallized their sense of society as a whole.

So, now, the air of abandonment, of waiting for some undeclared
future, which seems to lie over these neighbourhoods, reflects an
uncertainty about what to do, an inability to translate understanding into action, whose causes and dilemmas have a wider
relevance. In both Britain and America, successive governments
havè initiated special projects, redevelopment schemes, employment and training grants, community enterprises and organizations,

experiments in social service all designed to reverse the economic and social decline of the inner city. Yet taken together these interventions do not add up to a coherent or consistent understanding of the causes of decline. They seem superficial, irrelevant, ineffectual or at best to displace the problems somewhere else. But, conversely, as people working in urban communities have come to understand their problems better, and seen further into the causes of unemployment, deteriorating environments and social disintegration, they have felt increasingly at a loss what to do. Once the social and economic decay of a neighbourhood is set in the context of the far-reaching forces which shape it, the scope of the problem seems to overwhelm any power to intervene.

This difficulty of matching understanding to social action is my central theme. The theme has two parts. The first concerns the disparity between the scale on which economic resources can now be utilized and directed, and the scale of social and political organization. The sense of impotence underlying community organizations and struggles, even when they wrest a concession; the frustrations of urban policy, reflect a broader frustration at the inability of nations to govern the social consequences of the internationally integrated economy on which they depend. The second part of my theme concerns the way in which these problems come to be articulated in theories, analyses, ideological interpretations, which give rise to new conceptions of social action, but also to new inhibitions. The integration of understanding with action depends not only on knowing what we are up against, but on the language and conceptions into which we translate that knowledge.

In the course of this inquiry, I have tried to interweave these two aspects of the relationship between meaning and action. The next two chapters discuss two British attempts to revive deteriorating inner city areas - first, the Home Office Community Development Project, which involved twelve localities, and second, the plans to redevelop London's Docklands. I explore how administrators, researchers and community organizers struggled to define effective strategies of action; and how, as the analysis of urban problems evolved through experience, the connection between understanding and action became harder and harder to make. No practicable starting point - either in incremental or experimental reform, or in organization for more radical change - seemed to engage convincingly with the structure of relationships from which the hardships of inner city communities arose.

The history of these projects and plans illustrates how reformers and more radical or militant advocates of change relied on each other to sustain a context of ideals, to which both could appeal for broad support, however bitterly each might accuse the other of betraying these ideals by their tactics. But this context cannot any longer be taken for granted. In the fourth chapter I have tried to show how the changes in economic structure, which underlay the decline of city neighbourhoods, and the policies of government which reacted to them, have led to conflicts of expectation and contradictions of purpose which the progressive, liberal ideology of the past thirty years can no longer master.

Chapter 5 explores the alternative new conceptions of policy emerging from this dangerously volatile ideological disintegration. By analogy with Thomas Kuhn's sense of scientific paradigms, I have tried to set out the two competing sets of principles upon which social policy could now converge, each representing a profoundly different understanding of the problems, the kinds of government and of knowledge needed to solve them.

The next chapter takes up the question of how a new paradigm, when it presupposes a radical change in the nature of government and command over the economy, can be translated into the practicable strategies of social movements. The difficulties are conceptual, as well as political: the analogies which a language of explanation suggests help or hinder the process of defining actions which made sense. The terms in which economic, political and ideological changes are understood and the explanatory models adopted to interpret them in themselves influence the possibilities of action. Radicals - and increasingly, too, people more influenced by liberal, democratic traditions of reform - characteristically represent to themselves the relationships which underlie the persistence of poverty and social injustice in profoundly inhibiting and self-defeating metaphors. But these metaphors are not an integral part of what has been understood. They simplify and dramatize relationships which, when more fully described in different words, seem more open to change. Because the choice of language affects the choice of action, I have taken metaphors as a starting point from which to understand strategies of social change better.

These questions of meaning and action, of course, will present themselves very differently according to the actors, their situation and their preconceived ideals. Throughout this book I have been concerned with four groups of actors whose vocations are more closely bound up than most with articulating theory and practice: reformers who, within the framework of institutions, try to translate better social understanding into better policies; community organizers and advocates who interpret local struggles in the light of broader themes, so that these struggles can grow into a cumulative movement towards social ideals; social scientists who try to develop research as a means to resolve questions of action; planners who set out to synthesize, through the conception of a plan, some integrated strategy for matching social purposes to possibilities. All these play the part of intellectual mediators. They interpret particular situations and needs in the light of broader conceptions from which collective definitions of purpose and action can arise: and their authority to do this comes from their intellectual vocation, as people trained in the articulation of general ideas. So, for instance, they take up the claims of inner city residents for better housing, more jobs, less degraded surroundings, and justify them in terms of ideals and principles which the institutions of society claim to represent as a whole. Correspondingly, they try to rationalize a policy or a community movement in terms of their understanding of the whole complex of relationships which bear upon it.

This concern with the integration and generalization of social meanings makes them peculiarly sensitive to the disparities between theory and practice, ideal and performance. Their professional status within the institutional structure of society depends on what their constant search for solutions to the problems created by these disparities contributes to rationalizing and legitimating social relationships. They are valuable to the authoritative order of society because they help to articulate the practical and ideological adaptations which may be needed to maintain the basis of political consent. At the same time, they enjoy more ideological autonomy than most professionals, because without it they cannot discuss these critical issues of legitimacy. The difficulties of legitimating and rationalizing policies at first provoke new kinds of mediation and then undermine them as the ambiguities of these mediating roles become unmanageable.

In a sentence, then, this study is about the way in which some kinds of intellectual actors, in the circumstances of two British policies, tried to make sense of what they were doing, and what we can learn from that experience for the future direction of social change. It is written from the point of view of a broad democratic, egalitarian tradition of ideals, to which most of the actors in this book belong, as I do.

But before I come to the first of the policies I want to examine – the Community Development Project – I ought to explain why I believe this question of the *meaning* of social action is so important. One might argue that the rationality of actions is a matter of whether they match the purposes of the actors, on the one hand, and whether they are realistic, on the other, and that these are the only aspects of their meaning which can be critically analysed. For the rest, meaning is the expression of values, whose shared validity has to be resolved through a political process of competitive assertion and negotiation. Much evaluative analysis of social policy takes this stance: actions are reviewed in the light of their outcomes, and these outcomes compared with the stated purposes. Such research characteristically concludes by criticizing the vagueness and inconsistency of the purposes and the mistakes in the actors' own analysis of their situation. It implies that policies will make sense when the actors know their situation and define their purposes clearly. The intrusion of other questions of meaning into this assessment only makes it less clear-headed.

This approach treats purposes in a very artificial manner, as if they were plucked out of a repertoire of values which the actors are supposed to cherish independently of events. But purposes are as much an interpretation of previous experience, a response to the outcome of actions, as an expression of preconceived ideals. The rationality of purposes in the light of experience is as crucial and analysable a question as the rationality of actions in the light of purposes. So rationality, which might seem at first a less fuzzy and ideologically contaminated concept than meaning, cannot after all be abstracted from the constant, self-reflective reinterpretation of both our circumstances and our intentions, by which we try to make sense of our lives.

In the discussion of social policies or political strategies, the conclusions you can draw from matching actions against intentions, or assumptions against the experience of events, are only interesting or useful in some context of meaning which is itself constantly evolving out of this experience. That is, unlike an exact science, it is impossible to hold the theoretical framework constant while the outcome of some intervention is observed and interpreted, because the social equivalent of such a framework is a set of meanings which expresses the needs of living actors constantly adapting to events.

These meanings form and develop at many levels of generality, from the most intimate and personal to the abstractions of political ideology: and each level reacts upon others, as we both influence and are influenced by the collective meanings of the societies to which we become attached. But at any level, a structure of meaning attempts to organize the relationship between three aspects of reality: the observable associations between categories of events; the emotions these events provoke; and the purposes they entail. That is, it provides a framework in which to think about what is likely to happen, what it would feel like, whether we want it to happen and how we can influence it. Each of these questions involves the others: our intentions affect how we categorize events, these categories define the predictable relationships in whose terms we think about the future and so, reciprocally, influence our intentions; just as the feelings which events provoke at once reflect and shape our intentions, colouring the categorical language through which we represent experience. So, for instance, a group of people who set out to defend a neighbourhood from redevelopment will tend to categorize events and actors according to whether they are likely to help or hinder the neighbourhood's preservation. The more the group's attention becomes preoccupied with these strategic issues, the more all manner of events will be interpreted by reference to them; and this way of organizing reality may make the group seem more embattled, more diffusely threatened, so that it comes to feel victimized by the social structure as a whole. This may then lead its members to redefine their intentions as a struggle to change society rather than to defend a neighbourhood. This cycle of reinterpretation will continue to evolve. A structure of meaning can only artificially be broken down into components of causal, emotional or intentional structure: it is a self-reflexive whole - a conceptual operation by which an actor or a group of actors constantly develops an interpretation of experience.

The question of whether a form of understanding is capable of generating meaningful action is, therefore, much more than a matter of whether its predictions are confirmed by experience. It turns on the way in which the interactions between emotional,

intentional and causal inferences are characteristically organized
into interpretations. Some structures of meaning may be confirmed
only indifferently by events, yet capable of generating purposeful actions whose outcomes deepen understanding, while others
predict better, yet lead nowhere. Unless understanding leads to
actions and new experiences, nothing more can be learned from
it; and unless it can assimilate these experiences within its interpretive structures, the process of learning becomes traumatic.
The vitality and productiveness of the meanings which inform
policies and social movements depend, then, on qualities of structure of which rationality is only one and not necessarily the
most valuable.

Meaning, then, is I think best conceived of as a comprehensive,
integrative structure of interpretations which each of us elabor-
ates through experience and depends upon for confidence to act.
So, when we can influence events, we tend to foster relationships
which conform to that interpretive structure. Correspondingly,
when events cannot be assimilated to the structure, what people
do, and whether it helps or hinders their recovery of confidence,
depends on how the process of retrieving and reformulating a
sense of meaning works out. It is characteristically a painful,
emotionally exhausting process. When people can no longer find
meaning in their situation – whether because some crucial attachment which gave purpose to life has been lost, or because the
interpretive structure has been overwhelmed by events it cannot
grasp or contradictions it cannot resolve – the loss of any basis
for action causes intense anxiety and searching, from which new
meanings have to evolve. I have written in an earlier book about
this process of grieving, both as an individual and collective
response to loss, and I will not try to summarize that discussion
here,[1] but the universality and intensity of grief show how crucially we depend on the interpretive structures of meaning in
which our purposes, attachments, assumptions about reality and
our actions are inseparably bound up.

So I would argue, then, that we cannot learn very much by
evaluating social actions simply in terms of their effectiveness.
They can only be effective or ineffective from some standpoint of
attention which itself reflects a whole context of purpose and
understanding. We have to ask not only whether some action
succeeded, but how, in the light of events, ought we to regard
it: from what point of view, in what terms and with what feelings? What anyone learns from experience depends on the way
in which he or she answers all these questions – and since the
answer to each depends on the others, they can only be treated
artificially in any sequence of distinct inquiries. In this study,
therefore, I have tried to grasp the complexity of interaction between events and their interpretive contexts, holding the meaning of action at the centre of attention.

But there is another kind of objection to this concern with
meanings which I should take up briefly, because it helps to set
off much of the book's argument. Someone who agreed that

meanings were crucial to us, as social actors, and as complex in their structure as I have suggested, might still argue that they have little historical importance. So, for instance, the Marxist analysis of capitalism can be taken to imply that society evolves out of impulses inherent in its productive relationships, in a manner which is largely independent of how people of different classes or moral convictions represent these relationships to themselves. In every epoch, Marx himself writes, 'The ruling ideas are nothing more than the ideal expression of the dominant material relationships, the dominant material relationships grasped as ideas; hence of the relationships which make the one class the ruling one, therefore, the ideas of its dominance.'[2] Articulate, publicly expressed meanings are, then, the ideologies which rationalize and justify class interests. In the same passage, Marx goes on to comment on the part which intellectuals play in defining these ideologies, much as I suggested earlier, except that for Marx no fundamental conflict between intellectual mediation and the running of capitalist society is conceivable:[3]

> The division of labour . . . manifests itself also in the ruling class as the division of mental and material labour, so that inside this class one part appears as the thinkers of the class (its active, conceptual ideologists, who make the perfecting of the illusion of the class about itself their chief source of livelihood), while the others' attitude to these ideas and illusions is more passive and receptive, because they are in reality the active members of their class and have less time to make up illusions and ideas about themselves. Within this class this cleavage can even develop into a certain opposition and hostility between the two parts, which, however, in the case of a practical collision, in which the class itself is endangered, automatically comes to nothing, in which case there also vanishes the semblance that the ruling ideas were not the ideas of the ruling class and had a power distinct from the power of this class.

This seems to suggest that ideas, in themselves, scarcely influence the course of history. Ruling classes are overthrown by the evolving contradictions inherent in the material relationships they dominate, not by ideas. Intellectuals perform as a chorus for the men of action. What matters is not the meaning which people give to their actions, but the underlying structure of relationships, which determines who controls the resources to act - and whose ideas are reproduced. In this light, intellectual criticism seems rather futile. It will either be co-opted or ignored, until a different class gains access to these resources. The only important questions, therefore, concern the day-to-day struggle for power.

This revolutionary pragmatism is the counterpart of the style of policy evaluation that I criticized above. Both have an anti-intellectual bias, which relies on distinguishing between reality

and the meaning attributed to reality. And, of course, if we were
able to grasp reality independently of ideology, or of theory,
these structures of meaning would not be of much consequence
to the enlightened. But meanings can only be treated as ideological reflections of some more real structure in terms of some other
interpretive language, which also represents a conceputal organization of reality. We cannot examine our own understanding as
an ideological construct, since any language we might adopt for
the purpose - if we believe in it - is itself part of that understanding. So we cannot refer our ideas to the test of some impartial truth, unclouded by the illusions of desire, as we refer
the ideas of other classes, times and places to interpretation by
our own conceptual structures. For ourselves, the ideological
structure and the social structure are logically inseparable: we
cannot experience relationships except in terms of the categories
of meaning which make them intelligible to us. So while we can
see others as moved by events which they do not understand, we
can only see ourselves as moved by our understanding. Whenever I begin to see my ideas as a mere reflection of my social
situation, I have already abandoned them for another point of
view.

We have to treat our own understanding, therefore, as capable
of outgrowing the circumstances from which it sprang and of reflecting upon them. Otherwise we have no way of knowing how to
change them. Unless we believe this - and believe that others
can do it as well as ourselves - we become trapped in a form of
determinism which leaves the way open for highly authoritarian
structures. As Anthony Giddens writes:[4]

> A common tendency of many otherwise divergent schools of
> sociological thought is to adopt the methodological tactic of
> beginning their analyses by discounting the agents' reasons
> for their actions (or what I prefer to call the rationalization of
> action), in order to discover the 'real' stimuli to their activity,
> of which they are ignorant. Such a stance, however, is not
> only defective from the point of view of social theory, it is one
> with strongly defined and potentially offensive political impli-
> cations. It implies a *derogation of the lay actor*. If actors are
> regarded as cultural dopes or naive 'bearers of a mode of pro-
> duction', with no worthwhile understanding of their surround-
> ings or the circumstances of their action, the way is immediately
> laid open for the supposition that their own views can be dis-
> regarded in any practical programmes that might be inaugur-
> ated.

He goes on to emphasize that 'all social actors, no matter how
lowly, have some degree of penetration of the social forms which
oppress them'.[5] In chapter 6, I want to come back to this, because I believe it has very important implications for strategies
of change. The way in which we see the balance between social
predetermination and autonomy of understanding largely defines

the political opportunities that we recognize. Here I only want to show that no social theory can disregard questions of meaning without working itself into a position where people, as actors, become wholly absorbed into their roles and classes so as then to make it very difficult to explain how they ever escape from the conditions set by these positions, as they must if society is to change.

For all these reasons, therefore, I believe that the way in which people articulate their understanding profoundly affects what they do, and that the quality of this relationship between meanings and actions cannot be reduced to questions of reality, effectiveness or ideological rationalization. Unless we respect the autonomy of understanding, any critical study of social policy becomes either a polemical assertion of some particular under-standing, or a parade of illusions - and both lead towards author-itarian and self-defeating conclusions.

Yet I do not mean to underestimate the part which ideas play in rationalizing and legitimating the exercise of power. Structures of meaning are as much crucial determinants of social conformity as of change. They constitute the framework of assumptions with-in which authorities have to manoeuvre if they wish to avoid the legitimacy of their actions being called into question. Only revo-lutionary governments create their own legitimating meanings. For the most part, authority depends on a diffusely reproduced ideological framework which represents the relationships on which most people rely, for better or worse, in managing the social world that they take as given. This pervasive attachment to a familiar, predictable order is the greatest asset of estab-lished power, for it turns everyone, consciously or not, into an accomplice of its own confirmation.

These diffuse, convergent patterns of social understanding be-come, therefore, in themselves a powerful influence on social action, because they give rise to expectations which authority can only ignore at a cost to its legitimacy. If the expectations in which people have trusted are not met, they are less likely to take the exercise of power for granted. Government may then be forced to expose the coercive sanctions which underly its control: charges are trumped up, police called out, troops mobilized. But the resort to sanctions in itself changes the balance of power; because those who effectively control the use of force are never exactly the same as those who invoked it, and the outcome may be dangerously unpredictable to the present holders of power. The ideologies which legitimize government therefore also con-strain it. Because they reflect and justify the structure of control, the powerful too are bound by them: they are too diffuse and deeply embedded, too established in their institutional forms, to be manipulated at will.

Every act of government policy not only assumes this ideolog-ical support, explicitly or implicitly, but reinterprets it in the situations which come to be defined as problems in the light of that understanding. So government is constrained by assumptions that it cannot deny with impunity, while it constantly has to reinterpret these assumptions in new circumstances, finding a balance between tradition and innovation both problem-solving and legitimate. Ideological conformity is not represented by deliberate conservatism but by continual incremental reform within the framework of premises which are constantly restating a tradition of understanding. Making policy is a form of learning - the extension of a set of assumptions to encompass unfamiliar situations, so that these become intelligible and manageable.

If this adjustment cannot for the most part be convincingly brought off, the ideological structure underlying the processes of politics begins to break down. The legitimacy of successive governments becomes increasingly precarious, as they are caught between consensual policies which cannot satisfy expectations and divisive policies which attempt selectively to repudiate them at the risk of narrowing their constituency. Political alliances become less predictable. Groups who formerly supported each other's claims, asserting a common principle, become cynically competitive when they lose faith in the moral authority of government. So I would argue that the understanding of society which most of its members take for granted is a very important constraint upon the exercise of power, and its disintegration crucially influences the political context of action, even for those who, from their own ideological standpoint, never shared it.

This study traces the disintegration of one such ideological context through the experience of two policies which, small-scale and partly experimental as they were, confronted fundamental questions of the scope and meaning of political action in the highly developed industrial democracies of the capitalist world. It begins with the ideological preoccupations which administrators and social scientists brought to their conception of community development at the outset of an experiment that led them to unforeseen and troubling conclusions.

2 COMMUNITY ACTION

Ditchley Park is a gracious old country house in Oxfordshire, where the warden politely instructs American visitors in the niceties of English gentility - port is passed to the left, servants are to be addressed, tersely, by their surnames. Masterpieces of classical painting hang with dowdy dignity in the halls. You can walk through gentle pastures to the church, or play croquet on the lawn. In this characteristically remote setting, a conference of British and American social scientists and administrators convened in October 1969, to discuss programmes of social action and, more particularly, an experimental Community Development Project which the Home Office was about to undertake.

The conference had been conceived at a meeting between Richard Nixon and Harold Wilson in the previous year, and confirmed by a visit of the Home Secretary to the White House. In these discussions, it had been agreed that 'the two countries should look together at some of the domestic and social problems faced by their governments'.[1] This convergence of British and American approaches to the problems of social deprivation is the starting point of my inquiry. What did a Labour prime minister, committed to a conception of centrally managed, universal, and increasingly egalitarian social welfare have in common with a Republican president, whose country's welfare system was by comparison fragmented, partial and still imbued with many of the prejudices of the nineteenth-century English Poor Law? Why, especially, should British interest have concentrated on an American experiment in community action, which in eight years had demonstrated few achievements, frustrated its sponsors, angered both politicians and community leaders, and wasted so much of its intellectual and reforming energy in internal conflict? And why should such high-level attention have been directed towards an experiment which, even in the United States, was pitifully funded for its stated purpose of eradicating poverty, and which in Britain was to comprise twelve small community development projects among only 120,000 people?

In one sense the conference represented less a convergence than a succession. The Americans handed on an ideal with which they were already largely disillusioned: throughout the discussion they returned again and again to the inherent difficulty of carrying out a social experiment - the ambiguous and shifting purposes of reform; the divergent interests of clients, administrators, and scholars; the impossibility of rigorous method; and the immaturity of social science theory. Already in the United

States community action was being gradually but progressively
dismantled, and presidential policy was turning towards a national family assistance plan whose conception was closer to British
social welfare policy of the previous decade. Yet the British were
undaunted; it was only to be expected that the Americans had
made a mess of things, given the notorious political immaturity
of their society.

Behind this innocent arrogance lay, I believe, much deeper
reasons why, in both countries, the search for ways of relieving
social distress had turned towards local, innovative, experimental
intervention. Not only government, but more radical reformers
were adopting similar strategies in the name of community action.
Whatever the difficulties, there seemed no other way to go. The
provision of social welfare by public services or universal benefits ran up against the limits of practicable taxation to finance its
rising cost. Selective help to those in greatest need revived the
humiliating means-testing of the old poor laws. But a concentrated
effort on neighbourhoods where hardships seemed to cluster
would surely, if nothing else, break out of the dilemma of these
traditional alternatives, prospecting new possibilities of reform.
Hence community action was an experiment in a profounder sense
than merely the testing of this or that theory of social science. It
tested the vitality of reform itself - the faith that rational, democratic incremental intervention in a market economy would progressively secure a good life for everyone. Just as an apparently
trivial observation can undermine the theoretical paradigm on
which a whole scientific tradition rests, so a small experiment in
community action might put in question the underlying assumptions of liberal ideology.

This issue was never confronted by the conference, but it was
audible - a distant thunder rumbling behind the academic argument and placid thud of croquet balls. A.H. Halsey, research
director of the Educational Priority Area Project, introduced a
paper on government against poverty with this warning:[2]

> We might do well to reflect, before we are wholly committed to
> our plans, that it can be argued that no serious changes are
> possible in the present structure of rewards and opportunities
> without revolution . . . . However, what we have to talk about
> is the development of governmentally inspired and framed pro-
> grammes against poverty which are posited on the assumption
> that the welfare society may be attained through the legitimate
> use of the existing political structure. This assumption may,
> of course, prove historically to have been the most interesting
> facet of the Educational Priority Area and Community Develop-
> ment Projects. It may turn out to have been nothing more than
> a shibboleth of liberal society in decline.

His next sentence began with another 'however': such thoughts,
like scouts of a revolutionary army, skirted the discussion and
took cover again, never pursued. Yet, though the enemy was

scarcely acknowledged, the theme of the conference was defined
in strikingly defensive terms. From the outset, the Community
Development Project was presented as an attempt to vindicate
the adaptability and responsiveness of government, from the
point of view of a humane and dedicated civil servant, Derek
Morrell.

THE ADMINISTRATOR'S VIEW

Derek Morrell had promoted the Community Development Project,
whose aims and methods were the conference's central preoccupation. Two years earlier, he had begun to discuss with a few
colleagues in the Children's Department of the Home Office the
idea of 'community development areas', analogous to the Educational Priority Areas initiated by the Plowden Committee on
primary education. In selected areas, he suggested, the vertic-
ally integrated structure of social services, which met most
people's needs well enough, should be supplemented by a hori-
zontally integrated structure, designed to co-ordinate help to
those who had many more problems and were more severely dam-
aged by them. At the same time, these teams of workers would
encourage traditions of mutual support within these communities.
Morrell drew these ideas partly from Richard Hauser, who had
undertaken several experiments in community organizing in
Britain; partly from the Educational Priority Areas; and partly
from American experience of community action, which his col-
league, Joan Cooper, knew well. Behind this lay a deep, personal
faith in a Catholic sense of community.
   In April 1968, as Morrell and his colleagues were developing
their proposal, the prime minister announced a new policy of
grants for inner city areas with special needs, such as areas with
large immigrant populations. Fearing that their idea would be pre-
empted, they at once decided to emphasize its experimental character, so that it could be presented as a pathfinder for this new
urban programme. In that form, and now adopted as government
policy, Morrell introduced the Community Development Project to
the conference.
   But the crucial issue was not just how to adapt social services
to special needs. For Derek Morrell, as he made clear in his opening remarks, the underlying question was the legitimacy of government itself as an instrument of reform:[3]

   The general context, as he saw it, was the liberal-democratic
   process. It would be possible to discuss programmes and policy on the assumption that we had lost faith in this process,
   but he himself believed it had a highly creative future potential.
   Looking then at the assumptions about the role of government,
   or political process, it appeared to him that there were two
   principal ones to be considered. First, that the prime object
   of government was to maximize the total supply of welfare . . .

and second, to produce a more equitable distribution of welfare. Inevitably there was conflict between these two aims . . .
Some might take the view that only a socialist solution could
reconcile the two, but this basis was not open to the conference, whose task was to consider how progress could best be
made, piecemeal, along both paths simultaneously. Legitimacy
for a policy of reconciliation could be sought in the process
of gaining consent, and the painstaking accumulation of evidence. If this hypothesis was helpful, the role of the social
scientist or administrator was to generate consent. The role of
both was to find strategies of social action which would do both
of these things. There was no doubt that this was very difficult. The whole process was wide open to manipulation, and
involved the political problem of the transfer of power, from
the 'haves' to the 'have-nots' - power in the sense of the
ability to affect or resist change. Even success, in this process, might be dangerous and could destroy consent. But today's problem was not success, rather that consent might be
withheld, because of accumulating evidence of failure.

That was all he said: the discussion promptly took refuge in
methodology, and debated the criteria for evaluating failure. But
the statement itself expresses, almost casually and with extraordinary compression, a complex theory of government. From it
can be unravelled a set of issues about the legitimacy of government, and the interplay of its rational and democratic justifications; about the dilemmas of economic intervention, political
alienation, and the management of consent; about the possibility
of incremental reform as a means of redistributive justice and
transferring power. Community action, in both its American and
British forms, was directly concerned with these issues. It sought
to make government at once more democratically responsive, more
rational and more knowledgeable about the needs of the poor - to
integrate them into the political, economic and social structure so
that they would enjoy more of its benefits.
As Morrell saw it, the Community Development Project was to
explore a profound and far-reaching question: how were the needs
of economic growth (maximizing 'the total supply of welfare') to be
reconciled with its equitable distribution - in a society increasingly troubled by its lagging economic performance? But the field
of exploration was to be twelve scattered neighbourhoods, with a
budget of only five million pounds for five years - scarcely more
than eighty thousand pounds a year for each, from which both a
research team and an action team were to be financed. Clearly,
such an endeavour could not hope to influence economic structure. But it could discover how communities and local government
might adapt more successfully to that structure - and so generate a more willing consent to the constraints of a troubled economy.
The Home Office foresaw three lines of thought and action for the
Project to explore: a better understanding of social needs, closer
co-ordination of services, and community initiatives.[4]

The Community Development Project is a modest attempt at
action research into the better understanding and more comprehensive tackling of social needs, especially in local communities within the older urban areas, through closer coordination
of central and local official and unofficial effort, informed and
stimulated by citizen initiative and involvement.

Community Action in the United States had set out with very
similar ideals. The Grey Area Program, as the Ford Foundation
had conceived of it ten years before, placed its hopes in just
such a combination of co-ordination and community self-help, of
research and action. The Americans at the Ditchley conference,
with a decade of frustrating experience, warned of the inherent
ambiguities of the whole approach. Martin Rein - with whom I had
already published an account of the dilemmas in which the Ford
Foundation had become entangled[5] - ruthlessly outlined seven
flaws in the design. First, 'It was apparently based on the assumption that borrowed or seconded staff were a satisfactory
basis for an action strategy: all the evidence pointed to the dual
allegiance of such staff as predisposing a programme towards
disaster.' Second, 'The evidence suggested that special programmes of the kind under discussion were totally unsatisfactory as
a mechanism for achieving coordination, because agencies' autonomy was too well protected.' 'The third fallacy . . . was that of
believing that it was possible to separate research and action.'
(The CDP research teams were to be university sponsored, and
independent of the action team's control.) Fourth, marginal new
resources could not bring about substantial change. 'As soon as
the resources were committed, any leverage . . . disappeared.'
Fifth, 'Dependence on self-help as a means of supplementing
social service provision led, according to American experience,
to politicization of the social services.' Sixth, 'The British were
following in American footsteps in vastly overrating the universities' potential contribution to social policy; the willingness and
capacity of university personnel to contribute to policy making
was far too easily exaggerated.' And last, 'Evidence did not
overcome the commitment of people and agencies to traditional
values and process.' He concluded that the Project 'was likely to
suffer from being planned separately from regional economic and
employment policy; this reflected his own belief about the limi-
tation of effective coordination or improvement of service provision,
and of the underlying importance of economic opportunity for
success in improving social conditions'.[6]
These 'seven plagues' - as Morrell sourly dubbed them - were
disparaged as 'unconstructive' comment, confirming Martin Rein's
observation that evidence rarely overcomes a commitment to preconceived ideas. But if the British did not want to hear of
American disillusionment, it was partly because experimental
innovation in selected areas seemed to be the only practicable
strategy.
The neighbourhoods selected for the Project were to be charac-

teristic of declining industrial communities across the country,
where unemployment, decaying housing, and poverty seemed to
reinforce each other in a progressive demoralization. Their needs
could not be met out of any overall expansion of social services
and public housing: with an economy increasingly mortgaged to
international financial agencies censorious of public spending the
Labour government was finding it harder and harder to sustain
current levels of provision. Whatever funds might be spared for
special grants had already been allocated to the sixty-million-
pound Urban Aid Programme. Any further initiative would have
to be cheap; and as the American anti-poverty programme had
already seen, the only hope of progress without substantial funds
lies in the better management of existing resources: fitting them
more closely to needs, preventing their wasteful duplication,
evoking the latent ability of the needy to help themselves. For
this reason, the CDP formulation was to be repeated, again and
again over the next few years, in a bewildering variety of inner
city projects.

The British also believed that they could be wiser than their
American predecessors. They eschewed the inflated rhetoric with
which President Johnson had launched his war on poverty: here
was not even a campaign, but a 'modest attempt at action research', which need only produce some worthwhile experiments
in the co-ordination of social services to earn its keep. They
placed the projects unambiguously under the authority of local
government; in the tradition of a more elitist democracy, they
never felt that their legitimacy depended, as the administrators
of the American poverty programme had argued, on community
control. And the conception of research was less pretentious:
they did not insist, as the architects of both the President's Committee on Juvenile Delinquency and Model Cities programmes had
tried to insist, on elaborate preliminary planning as a theoretical
foundation for the testing of experimental action.

The British political setting also seemed easier to handle. Local
government had far less independence of national government
than in the United States. The structure of social services was
more uniform, more comprehensive, and more demonstrably a
national commitment to universal welfare. There were far fewer
semi-autonomous public or private agencies competing for jurisdiction and funds: the Community Development Project could build
upon the amalgamation and reorganization of the personal social
services recently proposed by the Seebohm Committee. The nation
as a whole seemed more homogeneous - without such a long and
bitter history of racial conflict, guilt and mistrust. So while the
Home Office representatives at Ditchley Park recognized the
dilemmas and ambiguities revealed by American experience, they
believed they could find a path through them - skirting, with
characteristic English wariness, the pitfalls of latent inconsistency.

But these seeming advantages were also liabilities. Just because
social services were more uniform, comprehensive and highly developed, they left fewer options for intervention, and because

local government was so closely controlled by the centre, the Home Office could not play off communities against City Hall, as the American Office of Economic Opportunity had sometimes been able to do to increase its leverage. National government could hardly repudiate the policies and constraints it had itself imposed. The modesty of the Project, though it might lower expectations, left open the need for more substantial policies: if Community Development Projects and their like were the government's only answer to urban deprivation, the feebleness of its strategy was exposed. In the United States the disappointments of community action could be blamed, variously, on the complex, constitutional divisions of powers, on the lack of a national welfare policy, or on the unwillingness of the poor to seize the opportunities placed in their way. None of these excuses could redeem the Community Development Project if it failed.

The two nations, though they converged on similar strategies, were coming from different directions. In the United States, Community Action represented the tentative beginning of a federal social policy - an intrusion into the traditional responsibilities of local government, hedged with acknowledgments to local autonomy. As it developed, its less controversial initiatives were absorbed into the structure of federal government as national policies, for which the Community Action Agencies were local agents. But once federal responsibility was accepted, it opened discussion of a national welfare system, a national health service - the kind of comprehensive insurance against hardship which Britain had already, in principle, instituted. By contrast, the Community Development Project was a reaction to the failure of that system - a search for a way out of the impasse of rising social costs and declining economic performance; not the beginning of national responsibility but an attempt to displace the burden on to the ingenuity of applied social science. In this sense, however unpretentiously it was presented, the Community Development Project and the inner city action-research strategies which followed it carried a heavier load of expectations than their American counterparts. If they could not find a way, what direction was there left to take but revolution, or a demoralizing palliation of incurable social hardship?

The conception of the Project was, therefore, at once tentative and unassuming, as befitted a small-scale experiment in the management of needs, and yet directed towards the deepest, most intractable issues of social justice. Its setting was the conflict between equity and growth, in an economy dangerously close to international bankruptcy. Neither rich nor poor would gain if the cost of social welfare priced Britain out of the market or drove investment elsewhere; and merely to sustain present provisions was proving harder and harder. Yet the social services had failed to protect millions of men, women and children from being deprived of proper housing, wages, education, or hope of achieving them. So any solution would have to depend on using resources more efficiently. But if people were to accept it, the solution

would also have to seem fair, and fairness meant satisfying legitimate expectations. Hence the task was both analytic and political:
first to discover what the best practicable reconciliation of social
welfare and economic necessity might be; and second, to per-
suade people to accommodate their expectations to it. Social
scientists, administrators and politicians, as Morrell insisted,
were inextricably bound together in the liberal-democratic process of generating consent.

I have presented the Community Development Project through
the mind of Derek Morrell, taking his phrases, setting them in
context, and reading into them what I think he implied, because
in the interplay between meaning and action, he played a crucial
part. As the administrator who inspired the Project, he mediated
between political purpose and its implementation, translating the
ideology of politics into concepts which both set the Project on
its course and justified his own role. Presidents and prime ministers are concerned with power: how to husband it and use it so
that it is neither wasted nor taken from them. They worry about
the ends of policy and the means of politics; the means of policy
they leave to their advisors. But administrators, in matching
political purpose to practicable policies, hold the power to shape
and inform that purpose with their own sense of reality. To
Morrell, that power seemed legitimate only if it was based on objective evidence. The administrator mediated between politics and
science, adapting each to the other.[7]

> The administrator was not so much the possessor of power as
> of skill, and what he wished to know was how to legitimate its
> use . . . . New policies needed an authority derived not only
> from political consent, but also from empirical evidence of their
> utility. Whether as advisor, or decision-taker, the adminis-
> trator should be enabled to make predictions about the outcome
> of policies by reference to evidence provided by social scien-
> tists . . . . It did not matter that success could not be abso-
> lute or that policies lacked the clarity or precision of academic
> standards. The process of searching matched with a concern
> that the search should be as scientific as possible were the
> fundamental points . . . .
> As an administrator he asked help from the social scientist,
> and in return he offered it to them to develop their role . . . .
> The fact that a conference had been held indicated that there
> was at least some community of purpose. This might be re-
> garded as the starting point, and not the end point of the
> dialogue.

With these remarks, he drew the conference he had dominated
to a close. Like a cherubic headmaster, firm in his faith, reprov-
ing the pessimists, negotiating the awkward turns of the discussion with the prep-school phrases beloved of English civil
servants, he had doggedly pursued his central point: politicians,
administrators and social scientists were bound together in a

3

search for legitimacy, without which they and the society they
represented would be lost.

Derek Morrell died two months later. Thereafter, no one at the
Home Office ever held together the strands of meaning by which
he had drawn administrator and experimenter in a shared endeavour.

Restless reorganizations, temporary assignments and changes
of staff robbed the Project of consistent central guidance. Apart
from a part-time Director of Research, distracted by other responsibilities and diffuse calls on his advice, no central research
team was established for eighteen months. But research was
crucial to the meaning of the Project, as Morrell had conceived
of it; and once the teams and their Home Office guides began to
define their experiments, they came up against a fundamental
flaw in his argument. Research legitimated policy because it provided incontrovertible evidence by which to predict and choose
the best course of action within some agreed but very general
context of need. But even if social science could find such evidence, its search was guided by theory; and theory was itself
ideologically controversial. The answers might be respectably
objective: the questions depended on assumptions derived in
part from the traditions of an academic discipline, and in part
from personal prejudice. Hence you could not derive an agreed
research programme from a broad definition of social issues, as
Morrell had hoped, once competing assumptions about the nature
of those issues had to be acknowledged. In search of a foundation
for the meaning and legitimacy of the administrator's function, he
had idealized the authoritative neutrality of social science. Coherent research depended on a choice between competing assumptions of relevance and probability. But what legitimated that
choice? If the administrator gave direction, the whole process
was circular, and the claim to have legitimated policy through research a hypocritical manipulation of scientific pretensions. So
even if the Home Office staff had been less disoriented, they were
inhibited from assuming control. Unlike their American forerun-
ners, they had built no particular theory into their design.

Paradoxically, the American programmes had been able to exploit social science more confidently because they were less
dependent on its legitimating authority. All of them instituted,
in one way or another, boards of control representative of the
community to endorse the experiments. Hence the originators of
the programmes felt free to suggest approaches. But the Community Development Project did not allow for any devolution of
democratic control, and in guarding its role as the responsible
mediator between knowledge and action, the Home Office gave up
the right to pre-empt the role of social scientist. Ironically, by
holding back from grass-roots democracy, it let the Project drift
towards a far more radical point of view than the American programmes ever countenanced.

THE RESEARCH DIRECTOR'S VIEW

In these circumstances, the one member of the Home Office
team with some authority to define the theoretical issues was
John Greve, the Research Director - an established and
respected professor of sociology at Southampton University. He
had already presented his strategy to the Ditchley conference,
and developed it as a short but comprehensive guide for the
Project teams.[8] In many respects, it was noncommitally inclusive: research was to inform the choice of action, monitor progress, and evaluate the whole endeavour. The findings might
be published in newspapers, academic journals, in reports to
government or voluntary agencies, or informative leaflets. The
research teams should take account of the whole range of demo-
graphic, social, economic, physical, pathological and institutional characteristics of the field, and, in exploring the consequences of intervention, be sensitive to the effect on people,
institutions and the projects themselves, to unintended outcomes, costs, and the interplay of values, evidence and judgment. In short, they should be all-knowing and all-wise.

Yet, despite its inclusiveness, Greve's paper took for granted
three established conventions of scientific method. Research
and action were distinct activities, to be divided into complementary but separate teams; otherwise research could not sustain its critical, evaluative function. And if the findings of the
twelve areas were to be co-ordinated, their methods of analysis
must be comparable. Therefore, an agreed set of indicators of
success or failure was crucial. Thus, without committing the
Project to any explicit theory, the paper implied consistent
measurement; and in determining what was to be measured,
Greve accepted the assertions written into the Project's administrative conception:[9]

It assumes, first, that families suffering from chronic
poverty or dependence on the social services tend to be
found in large numbers in particular areas, such as those
suffering from urban or industrial decay. Secondly, it
assumes that 'more of the same', in the sense of providing
these families with more help through the existing pattern
of social services support, though no doubt useful, is not
enough. This assumption is closely connected with a third,
namely that there are immobilized or untapped welfare and
'self-help' resources in communities; and, if ways could
be found to release them through appropriate social action,
they might have a dramatic effect, far greater than their
apparent value, in reducing dependency on the statutory
services. A fourth assumption is that, among families suffering from multiple deprivation, there is a great deal more
need than is known to the social services, and that the
gap between actual and expressed need is caused to a large
extent by inadequate communication. Finally, an assumption

which is implicit in some of those already stated; namely
that the optimal methods of improving the standard of life
and welfare in poor communities are by no means completely
known.

At first sight, this seems to assert little more than the need
for greater knowledge. But it implies that the crucial problem
is ignorance of the resources and handicaps of families whose
defining characteristic is their presumed concentration in decaying neighbourhoods. Hence Greve's own preliminary set of
social indicators, appended to his paper, is heavily biased
towards indices of personal competence - health, family breakdown, child neglect, school attendance, delinquency, vandalism,
eviction for anti-social behaviour, dissatisfaction with employment, isolation, use and abuse of social services. Neither
income nor rates of employment were included. The choice of
these measures suggested, more single-mindedly that the ori-
ginator of the Project intended, that poverty arose from the
demoralization of families unable to make use of social institutions or train their children to do better rather than from the
disintegration of social provisions, or the consequences of
economic structure.
Morrell had defined the relationship between knowledge and
action as an administrator saw it. Greve played his counterpart,
seeking to define it as a sociologist. Both tried to mediate
between questions of fact and questions of value, so as to
legitimate their own part in policy-making. Administrators had
the skill to translate political purpose into policy design: they
needed social science to tell them if the designs would work.
Sociologists had a method of inquiry: they needed administrators to provide that method with a practicable purpose. But
just as Morrell evaded the heart of the problem, by idealizing
the objectivity of science, so Greve idealized the authority of
administrative conceptions. He used the assumptions of the Project as justification for a comparative method which sociologists
understood, choosing measures familiar to them, from which
analysis, testable experiments and evaluation would emerge.
But his interpretation read into these assumptions more than
they meant to claim. Sociologist and administrator each looked
to the other for an authority secure from debilitating ideological
debate.
In the event, the Project teams were not prepared to accept
the control implied by a central co-ordination of research, either
in its method or implied theoretical approach. Some rejected
even the distinction in principle between research and action.
After two years of tense and deepening ideological questioning,
harassed by distracting administrative chores, John Greve withdrew and the central research team was disbanded. Thereafter,
whatever coherence the Community Development Project could
achieve rested with the initiative of the twelve teams themselves.
The communities selected for experiment included village and

small town as well as inner city, and they ranged from com-
paratively poor to prosperous regions of the country, but they
all represented, in one way or another, the costs of industrial
change and shifting patterns of economic investment: two
neighbourhoods in the East End of London, where manufacture
and jobs had been rapidly running down; a Welsh mining village, where the pits had closed; an isolated town in the Lake
District, with much long-term unemployment; and inner urban
neighbourhoods of eight Midland and Northern cities where
industry was in decline, jobs disappearing, housing conditions
were bad and recent immigrants were often concentrated.[10] In
each of these settings, under the control of the local authority,
but with funds provided by national government, the teams
were to try out ways of organizing services, housing improvements and community self-help, so as to make better use of all
the available resources. A corresponding research team was to
study what they tried to do, and draw lessons from it for
national policy. By 1972, most of these teams were in place.

Though the assumptions were looser, more tentative and open
to revision in the light of day-to-day experience than a scientific theory, the testing of ideas about social intervention remained
a central preoccupation. Very personal decisions about the way
in which to work raised fundamental questions: the search for
a relevant point of intervention had to explore the social context as a whole, to justify even a modest and limited strategy -
since the appropriateness of modesty was itself an assumption.
At the same time, the teams had to answer to an ambiguous
political mandate. Unlike civil servants or local government
officials, they had to meet expectations that were not defined
by any conventional structure of accountability. As professional
innovators, they were to influence that structure in ways which
they themselves had to determine. The evolution of the local
projects, therefore, can be represented as a continual search
for their own identity, setting out from the preconceptions of
cautious but idealistic civil servants to ask, as time went by,
more far-reaching and intractable questions.

THE PROJECT DIRECTOR'S VIEW

Within the shadow of Coventry's inner ring road, bleak brick
terraces of nineteenth-century industrial workers' housing
march grimly up a slope, broken here and there by wasteland,
where derelict cottages wait for their promised demolition. From
the rise you can see the new city centre: polytechnic, council
offices and cathedral - science, government and faith regener-
ated in monumental concrete from the ruins of wartime bombard-
ment. In Hillfields itself, modern blocks of cement flats poke
above the tiles and chimneys, hinting by their jaunty archi-
tectural touches at a lighter-hearted if equally monotonous
future, whose promise has grown fainter and more equivocal

through years of delay. Here in 1970 one of the first and most
influential of the Community Development Projects began to
explore its strategy.

Coventry was a controversial setting for an inquiry into
urban deprivation - a progressive manufacturing city, the
centre of the automobile industry, with faster growth, higher
wages and less unemployment than almost any other. But for
these very reasons, it offered the most favourable context for
concentrated local intervention. The city's government had
pioneered new styles of management and comprehensive redevelopment, and its economy was prosperous. Hillfields stood out
as a seeming anomaly amidst the prevailing air of purposeful
modernization:[11]

> known before the war as a respectable, well-established,
> cosmopolitan working-class community, by the start of the
> CDP experiment, the area had been run down badly and
> had developed a reputation as the city's blackspot, a centre
> of vice and crime, an area in physical and moral decline.

Its population - worse housed in shabbier surroundings than
most people in Coventry - included more pensioners, unsup-
ported mothers, unskilled workers, recent immigrants and
nearly twice the proportion of unemployed. Here, if anywhere,
a progressive local government, willing to experiment, ought
to discover how better to integrate a disadvantaged community
into the prevailing prosperity. And if the experiment were to
fail here, the prospect for teams in areas of general economic
decline - the Welsh mining valleys, Cumberland, Clydeside -
were discouraging. The Coventry project was also virtually
alone in running its full five-year course under a single director, with an established, integrated research team, and came
to acquire a position of leadership within the Project as a
whole. Hence its evolution represents the ideological dilemmas
of the whole experiment in its first five years more coherently
than its counterparts elsewhere.

John Benington, the director of the Coventry project, was
the son of African missionaries who returned to an austere life
in England when his father became an invalid. At the time of
his appointment, he had been a probation officer, working in
his spare time with a youth group of mostly West Indian boys.
Like several of the directors, he came to the Project doubting
the value of social work, aware how little probation officers
could understand their charges through professional contacts,
and increasingly preoccupied with the politics of the problems
he had confronted. But, like most of the other directors, he
had no preconceived theory of social intervention.

The position was at once seductive and alarmingly exposed.
He had access to senior administrators in local and national
government, an invitation to influence issues of policy; but the
nature of the experiment and his own part in it were wholly

undetermined. Was he to stand back, as John Greve's research
guidelines implied, while data for an experimental framework
were gathered and analysed? No research team had yet been
appointed – and was not to be established for over a year – but
even if it had, an intellectually rigorous strategy was impractic-
able. As the American programmes had discovered, research
and politically sensitive action set incompatible constraints.
Research turns upon the logical integrity of its method, and
reaches no defensible conclusion if action hurries on before
that method is in place, or dismantles it prematurely in search
of a more successful outcome. But action must respond to a
shifting context of expectations, frustrations, deadlines and
budgets where conceptions and strategies continually modify
each other to justify some realizable achievement. The history
of the Coventry experiment represents, therefore, not the
testing of a theory, but a serial redefinition of the theory to
be tested.

In search of a meaningful part to play, John Benington lacked
both the advantages and drawbacks of Derek Morrell and John
Greve. He had no professional identity – neither administrator,
social scientist, social worker, planner, management consultant,
nor politician – and hence no institutional definition to validate
his contribution and relate it, formally, to the social structure
as a whole. He was a licensed reformer, constrained only by
his zeal. But therefore he had to define himself in a far broader
ideological context, where the relationship between knowledge
and action, expertise and political purpose, could not be sub-
sumed under any given structure of jurisdictions. The legitimacy of his role depended on a comprehensive theory of social
intervention, in which the causes of poverty, the means of
change, the right to authorize these means and the value of
knowledge had all to be defined. Through five years of continued self-questioning he and his colleagues made and remade
taxonomies of such theories, charting the evolution of their
thinking, and laying them upon the Project as a whole, in search
of the moral and intellectual justification of their role.

At the outset, they accepted at least tentatively the assumptions implicit in the Home Office statement of purpose. The
social services were inadequate, because they did not fully
understand and therefore could not respond to need: Benington
had already seen, as a probation officer, how the professional
relationship disguised the true situation of his clients. People
wanted more advice on how to use services, more opportunities
to articulate their needs, and more means, through their own
efforts or those of government, to meet those needs. This
conception fitted the Project's design and scope and, whatever
their philosophy, most of the twelve teams acted upon it – with
information and advice centres, community playgrounds, day
care, neighbourhood workers, community associations and newspapers. But these practicable initiatives seemed both superficial
and fragile, unlikely to survive the withdrawal of the experi-

ment. They did not get at the community's two crucial concerns:
poverty and blighted housing. These called for long-term,
more fundamental intervention.

Hence the emphasis shifted from a dialogue over the provision
of services to broader planning. The model still assumed that
government and community shared the same interest in meeting
needs; the Project's role was to facilitate this dialogue, translating, researching, organizing meetings, articulating representation. But the team soon discovered the naïveté of this assumption: under the pressures of national government, industry,
the finance market, and its own budget, local authority was
more concerned to protect itself against the demands of a problematic and deprived community than to seek its advice. Whenever the issues involved the distribution of large-scale resources, government backed away from participation.

The team now faced the issue that had perplexed and divided
their American predecessors: in the last resort, did they work
for the community or local government? In effect, the Project
was responsible to neither, but had a vague mandate from
national government, which had pressed it on often reluctant
local authorities, and met three-quarters of its budget. John
Benington and his team responded ambivalently: they reformu-
lated their role as an advocate, rather than communicator, on
behalf of the community; but at the same time, they tried to
initiate reforms within the management of local government,
redefining policy issues, setting priorities, proposing innovative
decentralized social service teams. Research and experiment
were to be directed less at the weaknesses of those who received
services than at those who provided them. This redefinition
still assumed that local government was resourceful and open-
minded in principle, even if it was often clumsy and defensive
in practice. Senior officials, impatient with their own departments, were sympathetic; and national government could still
be persuaded that the strategy fell within its guidelines.

So far, the Coventry team had followed much the same course
as its American counterparts, balancing theories of poverty
as a vicious cycle of deprivation and incompetence which
demoralized distinctive communities, against theories of bureaucratic rigidity. Like the Americans, they discovered that the
disadvantaged were neither outstandingly incompetent nor unused to helping each other, and that the Project's own leverage
for institutional change was marginal. Not that the Coventry
Council was altogether unresponsive: services to the elderly
were much increased after the Project's research; consultation
over the redevelopment process was restructured; the Youth
Employment Service was stimulated to reconsider its assumptions
and practices; the decentralized social service team recruited
local residents, set up a shop-front office, and came closer to
its clients; schools became more imaginative and community-
minded. But these achievements only brought out more sharply
how superficial was the redress within the Project's means to

stimulate.
The final report concluded:[12]

> The main fields in which we have seen some responses are
> those of education and social services and there our joint
> programmes have contributed to some new thinking and to
> redirection or redeployment of staff in the field. However,
> even in these cases the changes have been largely limited
> to changes in practice at the field-level, rather than in the
> central policy making structures. This may be partly because
> 'People-processing' agencies like education and social ser-
> vices in some ways stand to gain (in the short-term at least)
> in the resources (e.g., professional man-power) allocated
> to them as a result of evidence of unmet need. On the other
> hand there is likely to be much more resistance to change
> in resource allocating agencies like planning and housing
> departments. Because they are rationing much scarcer and
> higher-valued resources (land and housing) evidence about
> unmet need is likely to create pressures for redistribution
> within existing priorities, rather than for any increase in
> the absolute level of resources available to them.
> In many fields, CDP's evidence and arguments about
> needs and problems were often accepted in principle by
> both politicians and administrators; but (in spite of the
> central government description of CDP as a pilot project
> for bigger developments later) we were rarely able in prac-
> tice either to deliver, or to channel, the scale of extra
> resources which our analysis implied, or to mobilize suf-
> ficient support (from our position within the administration)
> for redistribution within existing budgets. In these circum-
> stances it was all too easy for CDP to become institutionalized
> as 'the private conscience of the Corporation' providing an
> instant humanitarian commentary at every stage of decision-
> making, but impotent to influence the actual outcome on the
> ground.

In the United States, similar conclusions had led the experienced to argue, according to their politics, for either more or
less militant advocacy, research, central or local government
control, for more resources and fairer distribution or more
realistic expectations. Almost everyone still conceived of the
issues in terms of restructuring, in one way or another, the
interplay of applied research, policy-making, service provision
and democratic participation within the framework of governmental institutions and legitimate professional or political roles.
But John Benington and his colleagues doubted more and more
whether the frustrations of Hillfields arose fundamentally from
ignorance of need, incompetent planning, poorly provided
services or political insensitivity; or from the cross purposes
of scientific, professional, administrative and political endeavours. Compared with American cities, Coventry Council had

skills of integrated management, comprehensive planning, and
a capacity for large-scale development which most of them would
envy. For twenty-five years it had promised high priority to
the needs of Hillfields, and had long planned its comprehensive
redevelopment. Why, then, was the neighbourhood still deteriorating?

Benington saw the government of Coventry neither as a political compromise between competing interests, nor as the expression of a dominant clique, but as a management system, caught
between the policies of central government and the demands of
the economy on which the city's prosperity depended. The council had to provide the physical and social infrastructure of an
expanding engineering industry - roads, sewage, water, new
housing, schools, community facilities - within the constraints
of central government allocations and the financial market. And
the more sophisticated it became in handling these long-term
investment decisions, the more it resembled a corporate business
enterprise, dominated by managerial expertise rather than political representation:[13]

> The forms of organization which are prevalent in corporate
> management tend to centralize and unify the officer struc-
> ture in relation to elected members, and to shift the balance
> of power and prestige even further towards managerial and
> technical experts....The management techniques which have
> most commonly been introduced as part of corporate manage-
> ment (programme budgeting and operational research) were
> both originally developed as tools for management in private
> industry and in the defence industry. They are relevant as
> methods of coordinating long-range plans and financial pro-
> grammes, and for monitoring the production of the local
> authorities' goods and services, and for controlling the bud-
> get. It is less easy to see their relevance to the development
> of political strategy.

Businesses can be conceived of as organizations with simple
primary purposes, acting within a given environment. When the
theory which guides their management is translated to government, it tends to impose the same conception of a system within
boundaries, discriminating optimal choices. But in government
the boundaries of the system and its purposes are questions
of continual controversy. Corporate management, therefore,
tends to disguise political choices as organizational constraints.
John Benington became more and more convinced that the constraints which influenced Coventry Corporation represented a
systematic discrimination against the poor, deeply embedded in
the governmental and economic structure.

The final report of the Coventry project sketches the outline
of this analysis as its crucial conclusion. Essentially, it argues
that the management of economic uncertainty tends to displace
the whole burden of fluctuating demand upon the weakest,

whose marginality becomes necessary to the structure as a
whole. The stronger an organization or group, the more it can
manipulate events to protect the reliability of the relationships
which sustain it at the expense of others. The core structure
remains intact, insulated from the unpredictability of the market, while the weakness of those at its periphery is continually
reinforced by their vulnerability. The weak cannot increase
their control over their lives because the conditions of control
have been pre-empted by those who direct where the consequences of uncertainty fall. The structure of labour, of manufacture, government expenditure and space all reflect this
pattern.

So, for instance, the report argues that the largest manufacturers in Coventry cushion themselves against fluctuations
in the market by sub-contracting, displacing the uncertainties
on to smaller firms by varying the amount of work they contract
out. Correspondingly, within a firm, the workforce is organized around a relatively stable technical and administrative core,
while the unskilled are most immediately and most constantly
exposed to the vagaries of demand. Hence both the unskilled
and the workers in small firms are more vulnerable. Hillfields
held more of both than Coventry as a whole - the heaviest concentration of unskilled or semi-skilled workers in the city, with
fewer working for the largest engineering firms which dominated the region, 'a pool of low paid labour which local firms
hire and fire at will'.[14]

This economic marginality was reflected, not only in employment, but in its deteriorated housing. Public housing in Britain
is peculiarly vulnerable to manipulation in the interests of
overall economic management. In response to economic pressures, central government can regulate the rate of capital
expenditure more readily, and with less political outcry, than
it can cut services or raise taxes. Of all capital expenditures,
housing is the most adaptable, because the unit of construction
is relatively small. Government cannot very well leave a hospital
half-built, but it can, and often does, leave a housing project
half-finished, perhaps for years. Hence public housing programmes are continually at the mercy of national economic policy.
Central government can manipulate the capital expenditure of
authorities, turning back the management of uncertainty to
the weaker government, insulating itself in part from the political responsibility. Local authorities, in their turn, must
choose which amongst their projects can be adjusted with least
damage to these national constraints. They are likely to post-
pone those which will contribute least to their revenue or to
the economic prosperity of the city as a whole; which do not
involve the co-operation of private developers who might
become discouraged by delay; where the value of what is
already built does not depend on timely completion; and where
disappointment is politically manageable. For all these reasons,
whatever the commitment to decent housing for the poor and

unskilled, the practical pressures to make cuts somewhere tend
to converge upon neighbourhoods like Hillfields. Once again,
the consequences of uncertainty are borne by the weakest:
houses are abandoned, boarded up for demolition, then linger
like uncollected garbage; streets are torn down and fester as
wasteland; new blocks of homes rise out of bleak devastation,
awaiting funds to landscape their surroundings. The residents
cannot even make the best of what they have, because the old
homes have no future, and the future is beyond their control.
Uncertainty becomes more demoralizing than neglect.

Hillfields had lived with the blight of unfulfilled promises for
twenty-five years, its comprehensive redevelopment rephased
with every national economic crisis. As time went by, even
the promises became more ambiguous. Once the city centre was
rebuilt, the land which slopes down to it began to stand out
as the last remaining undeveloped central area. As the inner
ring road cut into the edge of Hillfields, sites along it were
pre-empted for industry. The area began to attract central city
amenities - shops, cinemas, clubs, a hospital, bus depot, foot-
ball ground, hostels for students. Thus the neighbourhood
came to represent, not only a reserve of labour, but a reserve
of land: an increasingly valuable reserve for the expansion of
the centre. But these new uses only dispossessed the people of
Hillfields, driving them into neighbourhoods nearby where the
same cycle of uncertainty and blight began again. They were not
only economically marginal, but continually trapped at the
physical margin of growth, where the undetermined potential
uses of their territory devalued investment in its present use,
compounding the uncertainty.

Hillfields, then, represents the slack in the system - the
reserve of land and labour, of social ideals and civic projects,
to be drawn upon or laid aside as the balance of economic activity allowed. Without a margin of reserve, no system of production can adapt to fluctuations in demand, and grow or change.
In a competitive, individualistic society that reserve is not inter-
nalized, as a cost which everyone shares, but is projected on
those least able to compete, who store the unused potential of
society, but cannot themselves realize its value. No market
economy has ever sustained for long the level and stability of
employment, or the steady predictability of demand and resources, to relieve everyone of this burden of marginality. The
hardships of neighbourhoods like Hillfields are therefore not
aberrant failures of social integration, but necessary consequences of the whole structure of private and public economic
management. The burden is passed on from stronger to weaker
until it comes to weigh on those people and places with least
power to displace it further. So, even if the people of Hillfields
could, by the advocacy of the Coventry team, by community
organization or their visibility as a national experiment, claim
the resources to rehabilitate their homes and surroundings,
and secure their income, they would only push the burden of

marginality somewhere else. Other neighbourhoods would suffer more from inconsistent funding and postponed plans, and there the least fortunate would end up. A few years later, as the economy of Coventry worsened, and unemployed workers began to lose their homes, the city government used the worst of its public housing, in the poorest repair, as just such a storage place for presently unwanted people.

None of the other Project teams carried their analysis to so devastating a conclusion, partly because they worked in areas such as the East End of London, the Liverpool dockside, a Welsh mining valley, a Northern mill town, where the economy as a whole was declining. In such places the problems of poor people could be conceived of in terms of regional inequalities - reversing the balance of investment between north and south, city and suburb - rather than as a necessary consequence of the economic structure as a whole. Though, if they had pursued the question of why these inequalities persisted, despite long-standing regional policies, they might have come to much the same conclusion as the Coventry team: the rationalization of investment both exploits and creates marginality in the interest of the organization's core structure.

THE PROJECT'S COLLECTIVE VIEW

All the project teams came to see employment and the quality of housing as the crucial issues, and concluded that both involved structural problems beyond the scope of community development. John Benington became increasingly involved in trying to draw these insights together. The first inter-project report, prepared largely at his urging by the English teams, concluded:[15]

> The problems of the 12 C.D.P. areas are not...isolated
> pockets suffering an unfortunate combination of circum-
> stances. They are a central part of the dynamics of the
> urban system and as such represent those who have lost
> out in the competition for jobs, housing and educational
> opportunity.

At the same time, as the twelve teams became increasingly dissatisfied with Home Office guidance, and the central direction of research, Benington, John O'Malley of the Newham Project and their colleagues in the other teams persuaded the Home Office to fund an information and intelligence unit, under the auspices of the Centre for Environmental Studies but guided by themselves, to co-ordinate their common concerns. The publications of this Unit dealt almost entirely with issues of national policy: public housing, the fiscal structure of local government, cuts in social services, and above all the consequences of the continual concentration and reorganization of

capital. 'The Costs of Industrial Change',[16] for instance, traces
the growth and decline of industry in five of the CDP areas,
showing not only how the closure of obsolete docks, textile
mills and heavy engineering works undermined the economy,
but also how the rationalization and concentration of contemporary industry makes use of this decline. Firms are bought up
and closed to eliminate competition; new investment in declining
regions may stay only long enough to secure the benefit of
subsidies; while high unemployment and cheap, old, abandoned
premises attract warehousing and marginal enterprises offering
low wages for unskilled work of low productivity with an unpromising future. And the distress of these declining areas is
only the most evident consequence of the spreading marginality
of the national economy within the world market. The report
concludes:[17]

> These declining areas have little chance of being 'regener-
> ated' again. There is so little mobile industry at present
> that a successful 'work to the workers' policy is nothing
> more than a liberal utopian dream. The irony here is that
> in this situation the competitive bidding by development
> agencies and local authorities continues on an increasing
> scale. When there is scarcely any mobile industry to cajole
> and bribe, there are more potential bribers in the market
> all doing the same thing, all with an even smaller chance of
> achieving any sort of solution to the problems.
> Nor is this the only contradiction in policy. While the
> government invents even more 'special' programmes, it
> abandons the very policies that might really begin to cure
> the problems of the inner cities and older declining areas.
> The most relevant measures are not to be found in tinker-
> ing with housing or labour markets, nor with population
> dispersal policies, nor in the creation of special develop-
> ment agencies or of regional assemblies – but with measures
> designed to control the activities of capital....Until policies
> are implemented which seriously challenge the rights of
> industry and capital to move freely about the country (not
> to mention the world) without regard for the welfare of
> workers and existing communities – who end up carrying
> the costs under the present system – the problems and
> inequalities generated by uneven capitalist development will
> persist.

So, as the twelve teams explored the physical and social
decline of their constituent neighbourhoods, they turned from
concerns with social services and community organization to
planning and the reorganization of local government, and finally
to a radical critique of capitalist economic structure. As they
were progressively disillusioned, they pressed the analysis
wider and deeper, until they did indeed conclude, as
A.H. Halsey had half-jokingly prophesied, that the assumptions

on which the Community Development Project had rested were
'a shibboleth of liberal society in decline'.

The Home Office, understandably, had little use for a radical
analysis implying far-reaching socialist policies, whose only
sympathizers close to government were the left-wing minority
of the parliamentary Labour Party, and their influence had
waned with the demoting of the National Enterprise Board and
Britain's entry in the European Common Market. It could not
suppress the findings outright, without seeming a clumsy cen-
sor of the research and experiment it had claimed to need. It
let some projects work out their time, brought others to a
premature end; grudgingly, under pressure, it allowed the
Information and Intelligence Unit to complete its series of
publications; and ignored the whole message. Meanwhile, new
inner city programmes and policies proliferated, all resting on
the assumptions whose inadequacy the Community Development
Project had struggled to expose.

But the teams themselves were divided and confused as to
what to do with such an analysis. In the first place, their conclusions could not claim the authority of a proven hypothesis:
they could not even show, unambiguously, that community
organization and innovative services were ineffective. Most of
the projects had succeeded in establishing useful amenities -
legal and advice centres, subsidized bus services, playgrounds,
community newspapers, street improvements, more imaginative
school curricula, and many had influenced local authority planning or departmental attitudes. They were disillusioned partly
because these successes demanded so much effort for such
superficial and fragile gains. Local authorities were seldom
wholeheartedly committed to these innovations, and even the
most demonstrably successful were liable to be closed down once
central government funding came to an end. The teams sus-
pected, too, that the gains were won only at the expense of
other, equally disadvantaged people. Hence their conclusions
represented the judgment of experience, a personal assessment
of where the energy for change should be directed, rather than
the findings of research. The teams' final reflection on the
experiment as a whole, 'Gilding the Ghetto',[18] scarcely discusses
the Community Development Project itself, but reviews a decade
of inner city anti-poverty programmes with impatient contempt
for their repetitive futility. The collages of newspapers cuttings,
scenes of industrial dereliction, graffiti, posturing public
personages which illustrate its arguments are designed as much
to wither the pretensions of liberal ideology as to picture the
setting. As a whole, the collective conclusions of the Community
Development Project were more concerned to change the underlying conception of the issues - to present new definitions of
the problems and new hypotheses to test - than to evaluate the
work they had done. Hence, however grounded in experience,
they had only the authority of personal conviction; and they
changed the ideological framework of discussion so radically

that there was no longer an institutionally definable audience
to address, nor a legitimized role to play, whether as social
scientist, consultant, community organizer or planner.

All the projects therefore faced the dilemma that if they
followed the structural analysis to its conclusion, they must
abandon the institutional setting in which alone they could
legitimately claim government attention for their findings. In
practice, therefore, the final recommendations of each team
tend to back away from the implications of their argument.
Even Coventry's report - the most unequivocal and far-reaching
in its analysis - ends by linking this analysis to a set of recommendations at least notionally within the scope of a progressive
local authority: more involvement, along with trade unions,
in the decisions of local firms which affect the community; more
use of public employment to offset redundancies; more consistent, predictable redevelopment planning; legal advice centres;
services for the elderly and the social development of the young;
the provision of knowledge and technical skills to strengthen
the political effectiveness of community groups; pressure on
central government for fiscal reform and greater resources to
help the poor. These recommendations imply that a combination
of advocacy, community organization and services can redress
the balance of advantage. But the body of the report insists
that the blight of marginality is an integral consequence of the
whole structure of public and private investment; and hence any
gains from advocacy can only displace the hardships.

Similarly, the London Borough of Southwark team discusses,
again and again, the council's inability to respond to even
modest changes of practice which might relieve the 'enormous
dissatisfaction at the uncertainty of the position in which the
people of the area find themselves'.[19] This uncertainty arose,
as in Coventry, from the continual postponement of the redevelopment plans. The team proposed an official Working Party
to draw up a definite schedule of construction. The proposal
was accepted; a carefully considered redevelopment strategy
was prepared; a date for construction was confirmed - and as
it was due to begin, postponed without consultation for another
year. 'The consequences of this decision completely destroyed
the original raison d'etre of the working party.'[20] Nor were the
members of the working party even informed that it had been
taken. Yet despite such experiences, the Southwark report
ends by recommending a sweeping reorganization of local
government which seems, in the light of this history, naively
Utopian.

Only Liverpool, of all the twelve teams, acknowledged unambiguously that the mandate of the Project could not be stretched
to take account of a radical structural argument. It did not
deny the argument: the Vauxhall neighbourhood of Liverpool
was 'among C.D.P. areas, in many ways the extreme case of
these structural problems, with unemployment levels reaching
an estimated one in four workers, and one in three in the

younger age groups...'.[21] It had suffered the characteristic
disintegration of a community[22]

> crippled by...the decline in Liverpool's importance as a
> port and the closure of related industries; fragmented by
> the dispersal of its population through clearance and
> redevelopment programmes; and finally carved up into
> isolated sections by new motorway and tunnel developments,
> its open spaces a convenient parking lot for lorries heading
> for the docks, or the cars of city centre commuters.

But perhaps because the situation seemed so desperate, rather
than question the relevance of community development to
these structural problems, the Liverpool team questioned
whether the problems were amenable to the community work
within their scope. They concentrated instead on what they
could hope to bring about by local endeavours, even though
'many of these are minor changes judged against the major
social and economic problems facing Vauxhall, and they may
have diverted resources from other needy areas of Liverpool'.[23]
All the teams, though they endorsed a radical analysis of
the causes of deprivation, tended to present their recommendations as if they were offering professional advice to government (though the teams who reported later, after the final
dissolution of the Project as a whole, wrote with more detachment). They differed from each other most in the professional
stance they took - some adopting the language of planning,
some of management-consultancy, some of community work.
They understood the problems in much the same way, and they
did much the same things, but they disagreed about the relationship between meaning and action. The Southwark team,
for instance, wrote as if a more drastic reform of local government would redeem and make sense of their disappointment
with milder changes. The Liverpool team lowered their expectations, regarding the implications of the structural analysis as
beyond their competence and their mandate. The Welsh team
discussed a better framework for regional planning.[24] The
Coventry team tried to steer local government towards a closer
alliance with trade unions and deprived communities at the
expense of business. Each could fairly claim, on the evidence
they shared, that the proposals of the others were unrealistic.
But all of them faced the difficulty of defining a legitimate
response to the problems as they saw them. They were professionals, without roots in their communities, with much better
paid and prestigious skills, and a broader, more theoretical
understanding than the people for whom they spoke. They
could not escape the part of mediators between the world as
policy-makers interpreted it and as local people saw it: and
so, to define themselves, they were brought back again and
again to the questions with which Derek Morrell had opened
the Ditchley meeting. What legitimates collective action? Is it

some combination of politically defined purpose, social research,
and administrative know-how? If so, in what ideological framework is that synthesis to be brought about? The Community
Development Project felt they had shown that Morrell's 'liberal-
democratic process' was an inadequate framework. As experimental teams engaged in action research, they could legitimately
present that finding. But they could not agree upon an alternative ideology of social action, because they were still preoccupied with rival definitions of their professional authority,
all derived from the ideology that they were explicitly or
implicitly rejecting. Planners, researchers, community workers,
management consultants depend on an understanding of their
moral responsibility, and therefore their right to intervene, to
seek clients and claim support, defined by liberal conceptions
of the legitimate structure of power. Once you see that structure as inescapably dominated by relationships which create
the problems you are trying to solve, you cannot adopt an
accepted professional stance within it. But without such a professional responsibility, you are left with nothing but a personal
commitment to seeking changes in that structure, without any
readily definable relationship to it.

The Community Development Project, in its team reports,
backed away from this dilemma, attempting - if sometimes half-
heartedly - to recover a professional stance. Only the collective
statement, 'Gilding the Ghetto' written by a group from several
teams, attempts to confront it:[25]

> For C.D.P. workers, the contradictions involved in being
> state employees paid to analyse the causes of poverty,
> meant that effective organization of all the twelve projects,
> across the institutional barriers drawn up by the Home
> Office, was essential both to protect our jobs and to extend
> our understanding of the problems we were employed to deal
> with. This has enabled us to develop our analysis of the
> reality which faces people in the areas of industrial decline
> and reject the definitions of the problems handed to us by
> the state. We have only been able to do this because at the
> same time we fought for the right to control our work - what
> we do, for whom we are doing it and why....For other state
> workers, working in the health service, public transport,
> education and other sciences, there are possibilities for
> similar activity once the contradictory nature of state ser-
> vices is recognized and the decision is made to work towards
> providing a service in the interests of the working class,
> not capitalism and the state. This means not just fighting
> against the diversion of resources away from the public
> services but also acting collectively to change the structures
> through which these services are provided so that both
> workers and consumers have a service which is geared
> towards their needs and over which they have control.

But this is more of a rhetorical flourish than an answer to
the dilemma. The project teams, for all their difficulties,
enjoyed more autonomy and more tolerance to initiate changes
than most state employees; and their assignment ended before,
or in the Batley project because, they attempted to challenge
authority. Their experience does not show what collective action
by regular departmental workers could attempt. The statement
implies that the providers of services can identify with a working-class struggle against capitalism, acting at once on their
own behalf and on behalf of all workers, without losing their
professional identity. But while they may join with other
workers to resist cuts in service which threaten their own jobs,
they are valued and paid by the state because they enable the
present structure to survive - they soften hardships, mitigate
inequalities, integrate the rising generation into society, regulate the provisions of benefits and constraints. So long as their
professional critique is directed at performing these functions
better, they have some power to make changes. Once they
declare their radical purpose, they destroy their value to the
institutions which sustain them. Hence whatever sanctions they
can apply through collective control over their contribution
to society are effective only so long as that contribution is
fundamentally supportive of the institutional structure. The
providers of public services cannot see themselves as workers
in the class struggle without disguising the ambiguity of their
professional interests.

Thus the workers in the Community Development Project, if
they were to act on their structural analysis, had to find
another way of relating to the structure of power, without
anything to recommend them but their conviction and commitment. Their sympathies lay with people struggling against
the hardships of insecurity: but they still had to find a way
of mediating between the immediate concerns of the unemployed,
the poor, the victims of bad housing and abortive redevelopment, and their own understanding of the underlying causes.
They needed a constituency to endorse their work, through
whom they could establish an antagonistic relationship to the
structure of the state. But to do this creates its own dilemmas,
as explicitly socialist activists, working outside the institutional
structure, had found.

THE RADICAL ORGANIZER'S VIEW

Notting Hill, in the London Borough of Kensington and Chelsea,
has stood at the margin between poverty and prosperity ever
since its farms were first built over by speculative developers
one hundred and fifty years ago. Pretentious houses, emulating
the fashionable squares and terraces of the south, intruded
amongst the pig farms, along the line of the railway, until they
confronted the meaner streets of workers' housing growing and

consolidating beyond them. Property speculators, from the
first, have gambled on this boundary between workers and
gentry - and when they lost, exploited their unsaleable ven-
tures as best they could by converting them to overcrowded,
run-down lettings to the poor. Correspondingly, the borough
council, amongst the richest in London, has consistently neglected the impoverished minority within its northern boundary,
using few of its discretionary powers of public housing or
compulsory purchase, in the hope that the private market
would ultimately redeem the whole borough and push the poor
beyond its borders. So the neighbourhood incorporates with
particular intensity the conflicts of London as a whole: conservative council against its working-class minority; property
speculators against tenants struggling for fair rents and reasonable repairs; West Indian immigrants against longer-standing
white residents; an entrenched local Labour Party against
radical activists. And for twenty years, since race riots drew
attention to it, the neighbourhood has attracted a succession
of community workers - Christian, socialist, professional and
amateur - seeking to resolve these conflicts.

Amongst these were Jan O'Malley and her husband John, who
was later to become director of one of the Community Development Projects in Canning Town, on the other side of London.
They were part of a small group of socialists, with a background
of experience in the Campaign for Nuclear Disarmament and
New Left politics, who came to Notting Hill in 1966 to set up a
community workshop, committed to helping local organizations
'fight to wrest from the authorities whatever they decide their
community requires'.[26] Jan O'Malley's interpretation of their
experience shows how difficult it was to integrate their conception of the issues with a coherent strategy of action, even without the inhibitions of government funding and misleading liberal
assumptions.

As socialists, the group were primarily concerned with actions
which would expose the underlying realities of capitalism; but
they were skeptical of mere propaganda, anxious to help as
best they could with the issues in which the people of Notting
Hill were engaged. The exploitation and harassment by landlords,
the lack of open space for children to play, the delays and
uncertainties of redevelopment, the intrusion of a motorway,
the refusal of the council to restrain property speculation or
provide public housing - all these gave rise to a loose network
of organizations, whose style combined bargaining with direct
action. Families squatted in empty buildings to discourage
speculators or draw attention to their plight. The private
garden in a square was broken open and commandeered as public
playground. Property auctions were disrupted by coolly out-
rageous bidding, forcing the auctioneer to close the proceedings:
or details of the true condition of properties to be sold, the
plight and determination of their tenants, were circulated
through the auction room in the exact format of estate agents'

information sheets. The opening ceremony of the motorway was
overwhelmed by a cavalcade of demonstrators, effectively closing it again. When a committee of the borough council disap-
pointed local residents by their unresponsiveness at a meeting
one evening, the doors were locked as they tried to leave,
and the unfortunate councillors were forced to listen to the
frustrations of their constituents the whole night through.

Jan O'Malley does not say exactly what part her group played
in all this. But behind the defiance, the carnivals and street
celebrations, lay much research into the conditions of houses,
the structure of property ownership, the status of development
plans: and once the issues had been dramatized, arousing
widespread sympathy, they had still to be resolved through
the negotiations they provoked. The group saw themselves as
useful, I think, because they possessed a tactical experience,
a knowledge of institutional structures and sources of information, which enabled them to relate local hardships to a wider
context of social pressures, and see how practicable demands
could be pressed.

As a whole, these tactics were at least as successful as those
of the Community Development Project. The leader of the
council might mutter about 'gangs of thugs' and protest 'I am
not making any bargains with these bloody anarchists':[27] but
he did. With a bad grace, authority conceded to defiance what
it had denied to complaint. The private garden was purchased
as a public playground; families were rehoused; the right to
relocation from the intolerably noisy houses by the motorway
was accepted; and above all, policy towards intervention in the
private property market changed. Between 1966 and 1974,
council housing in the neighbourhood nearly doubled, and
housing by not-for-profit trusts (largely subsidized by the
council) increased five times. In 1966, 82 per cent of households were tenants of private landlords; eight years later only
54 per cent. In these years, the borough's capital expenditure
on housing had gone up from one to six and a half million
pounds. From a stance of complacent indifference to widely
publicized property scandals, it had turned to policies which
would, over the coming years, secure most households in the
neighbourhood from the uncertainties of property speculation
and the risks of rack-renting.

Yet to Jan O'Malley, the achievements still seem frustratingly
unrelated to more fundamental changes. As families won their
battles for rehousing they dispersed, leaving no organization
or continuity of purpose behind them. Groups worked on their
particular projects, but could never combine into a concerted
attempt to define a broader movement for change. A People's
Centre had been created in 1967 to act as an open forum of
discussion, through which the various campaigns were to be
brought together. But no one had the authority to establish a
structure of organization strong enough to impose coherence
without veering towards the exclusiveness of a self-appointed
clique.[28]

Attempts were made to structure and restructure the working groups within the People's Centre but the disciplined
reporting back of the working groups was never system-
atized, partly because the role of Chairman was never taken
seriously. Also the debate on the membership of the Centre
or of the People's Association was never resolved. Taken
together, these factors contributed to the working of the
People's Centre being dominated by the shifting movement
of cliques, and to the meetings being dominated by the
most confident; those with the loudest voices, and the
greatest capacity to interrupt and hold the floor....The
license to speak at meetings was both completely open and
yet for many who lacked the confidence and capacity to
interrupt, completely closed. The extreme tolerance of all
kinds of attempts at disruption even when it took the form
of infinite harangues and monologues and even physical
assaults on others at the meeting meant that...as time went
on people grew weary of attending the political forum they
had valued since it was no longer a place to pool ideas and
broaden perspectives. The purges and exclusions began
and it was not a political forum any longer. Instead it was
the domain of one particular clique. So in the absence of a
constitution which could be enforced and a fresh forum
being set up, people withdrew to the working groups they
believed in.

The rivalries between community workers, the racial and ideological tensions, kept effective action to fragmented campaigns
over particular, immediate ends - and these needs were inevitably defined by the powers and resources of government, which
alone might be pressed to do something about them. Hence,
despite their radical style, the campaigns were in practice
directed towards the provision of amenities and housing within
the scope of established legislation and the resources of a
wealthy borough.
  This 'tyranny of structurelessness', by which the People's
Centre - like other informal groupings - degenerated from a
chaotic parliament to an isolated and intolerant rump, reflects
a corresponding dominance of structures. Both the people of
Notting Hill and the group of radically minded professionals
who came to their aid lacked any institutionalized relationship
to power. The local Labour Party, with no hope of ever governing the borough, was preoccupied with national issues. Hence
the residents were effectively disenfranchised, and too poor
to counter the manipulations of the property market with their
own resources. The radicals, disillusioned with conventional
politics and institutionalized positions, looked for an alternative
relationship to power in terms of class conflict, by working
directly for the victims of capitalist exploitation. But this was
an alliance of mutual weakness: the community had no sanctions
to bring to bear against exploitation except to disturb the

peace, and the radicals had no resources or influence except
their knowledge and skill. There was therefore very little around
which to build an autonomous structure of activity. Lacking
any power of their own, people could in the end, however
defiant their tactics, only appeal to government for help: so
their own actions were inevitably structured by the policies
and institutions which determined what help might be conceded.
Correspondingly, everyone who worked for the community found
themselves playing much the same professional role, to much the
same ends, irrespective of their ideology, though strategies
differed. Competition for ideological hegemony only disrupted
the fragile networks of co-operation, without changing the
practicable endeavours.

So, paradoxically, the struggles in Notting Hill were more
narrowly concerned with conventional reforms than the Community Development Project, just because they arose from a
more uncompromisingly radical base. From its equivocal position
within the structure of government, the Project could raise
much broader issues, relating housing, education, employment
and social services together in an analysis of political economy.
But neither could find a strategy of action corresponding to
that analysis. They were caught in a trap: to attempt structural changes, they needed to attach themselves to some political force able to assimilate their analysis and powerful enough
to act upon it. Such a force would have to represent a broadly
based challenge to capitalism. But the only institutions with
widespread membership and socialist traditions - the Labour
Party and the trade union movement - had accommodated to
working within a capitalist structure. Most other political movements were concerned with specific and immediate aims, where
a radical analysis seemed only to diffuse energy by raising
larger and more intractable questions.

The members of the Ditchley conference had faced the same
trap in reverse: to make changes, they needed to attach policy
to an analysis powerful enough to comprehend the causes of
deprivation. But such an analysis could not be contained in
the assumptions from which government, party politics, economic management, social science and professional practice had
evolved, and by which they were defined. So throughout the
history of community action, administrators, social scientists,
project directors, radical organizers were all insistently troubled by an irreconcilable disparity between purpose and action.
Those who defined actions in terms of their legitimate role
could not disguise, even from themselves, the compromising
ambiguity of their purpose. Those who defined their purpose
by their analysis saw the weakness of the actions left open
to them. Everyone was at once disillusioned and idealistic,
continually seeking an ideologically coherent relationship between
understanding and power, through which to justify themselves.
This ideological preoccupation seemed at times self-absorbed,
irrelevant to what would happen. Yet without a shared context

of meaning the drift of events could only become an aimless accommodation to the consequences of the past.

In both Britain and the United States, experience showed that research into needs, the reorganization of services, comprehensive planning, advocacy and even open conflict had not successfully reversed the decline of inner city communities. The most persuasive or disruptive demands attracted resources from competing needs, as authorities juggled their constricted budgets for the relief of hardship. At best, housing policies and social services could be pressed to become more responsive to local needs, more imaginative in their methods; and people could become better organized to look after their own interests, understand their rights, and present their case. All this was helpful, but often ephemeral – lasting no longer than a demonstration project or the presence of a paid organizer. It did not get at the causes of property speculation, loss of jobs and growth of dependence, or of local government's growing fiscal inadequacy. Even at its most militant, community action had not confronted directly the issue of control over economic investment. Its challenge had always been made to government, and so became preoccupied with the distribution of public goods – education, housing, benefits, compensatory employment programmes – rather than with the distribution and use of productive resources. If community action was to be fundamentally relevant, it had to be integrated with these larger economic concerns. But in what context of political organization could these issues be brought together?

Both Jan O'Malley, disillusioned by the isolation of community struggles, and John Benington, frustrated by the inhibitions of government policy, drew the same conclusion: the trade union movement is the only powerful institution conceivably able to assimilate a radical strategy of change. However it has accommodated to the constraints of a market economy, it has never in Britain defined its ideals by them, nor accepted responsibility for sustaining a profit-making system on capitalism's own terms. John Benington left the Community Development Project to work out a basis for community action with trade union support. Jan O'Malley and her group had tried in Notting Hill to enlist union help, and though they won only a few tokens of solidarity, she remained convinced that 'class struggle for greater control within the community must be seen as necessary and complementary to the struggle for greater control within the workplace. Only by closer integration will the maximum potential of working class action be realized.[29] But as some of the Community Development Projects had found out, trade unionists were not necessarily convinced of the relevance of community action to issues of industry and employment.[30]

If this integration is ever to come about, an entrenched spatial and institutional separation of workplace and living place will have to be overcome. The friendliness of a neighbourhood, its services and amenities, the sense of being comfortably at

home depend on assets which people control as producers and
distributors of wealth rather than as neighbours. But the use
of resources is decided in factories and banks, in corporate
and government offices where the compelling issues are wages,
security of employment, the return to investment, tax revenues
and budgets. The quality of life derives almost accidentally from
a competition between workers and management, firms, governmental jurisdictions, defined in much narrower terms of economic advantage. The rules for productive and bureaucratic
players alike turn their attention to strategies for winning,
where the gains and losses are in institutional power, and personal income, not in the quality of living places. People can
only buy, according to their means, whatever homes and neighbourhoods come out of this competition: the structure of power
cannot articulate a process of collective design.

The radical ideal of a working-class movement, therefore,
like the reforming ideal of social planning, seeks to reintegrate
community and economic relationships, so that the quality of
life can emerge as the central concern of any exercise of power.
Ideologies of space - the definition of territory, the way in
which boundaries are drawn and organized in hierarchies or
overlapping networks - then become crucial to how the process
of change is articulated, and to whom its purposes belong. I
will try to explore, in the next chapter, how these spatial
ideologies influence the meaning of action.

3 PLANNING IN DOCKLANDS

Administrator, social scientist, organizer and activist each
searched for a conception of community action to integrate
their own skills and ideals with an effective strategy; and they
were all frustrated. Derek Morrell's synthesis of political
purpose, administrative skill and experimental problem-solving
could not deal effectively with causes beyond the scope of
professional competence, as it was institutionally defined; and
so, despite his earnest preoccupation with the legitimacy of
policy, could not confront the underlying ideological choices
on which analysis and policy rested. On the other hand, a
radical analysis had no framework of organization powerful
enough to initiate an alternative approach. Community action
could only react against local government, whose policies continued to define the practical issues around which struggles
took place.

But these frustrations arose partly because intervention was
concentrated in neighbourhoods too small to contain the elements of structural change. The Community Development Project
set out with the assumption that the misfortunes of deprived
neighbourhoods arose largely from causes within them - whether
in the incompetence of their residents, or of the services and
policies which should help them. More radical organization had
concentrated, in practice, on struggles over housing and services where a neighbourhood could mobilize to act directly. Once
everyone - reformer and radical alike - came to accept that the
social problems of the inner city arose from changes in the economy which neither better housing nor services could remedy,
they needed a larger framework. As the understanding of the
problem changed, so the spatial boundaries had to change too;
and the way in which these boundaries were redrawn would
crucially affect how meaning and action might be reconciled.

Planning, because it deals explicitly with the relationship
between spaces and meanings, brings out these issues especially
clearly: and because it is also fundamentally involved in controlling the future, it is as much concerned with boundaries of
time and chance as spatial boundaries. In this chapter I want
to show, through the story of one attempt at inner city planning,
how boundaries form or dissolve meanings; and also how
vulnerable these meanings are, when they try to represent a
social whole more inclusive and more fairly balanced than corresponds to any single system of control.

FROM COMMUNITY DEVELOPMENT TO COMPREHENSIVE PLANNING

The Labour government's White Paper on policy for the inner cities, presented in June 1977, announced a new concern with structural intervention. It was influenced especially by studies of inner London, Birmingham and Liverpool, commissioned from planning consultants,[1] and reflects the same conclusions as the Community Development Project. Unemployment, the concentration of vulnerable unskilled workers, planning blight and the plight of poor people trapped in decaying surroundings are acknowledged to arise above all from the pattern of industrial investment:[2]

> The decline in the economic fortunes of the inner areas often lies at the heart of the problem. Compared with their own conurbations, the inner areas of the big cities suffer from higher unemployment at all stages of the economic cycle. In inner areas generally there has developed a mismatch between the skills of the people and the jobs available....The inner areas have long had more than the national proportions of unskilled and semi-skilled workers, the groups amongst whom unemployment is highest....The loss from the cities of a higher proportion of skilled than less skilled workers has made unemployment worse. Between 1966-71 only 15% of net migrants from Birmingham comprised semi-skilled and unskilled workers; from Manchester it was only 16%....
>   At the same time, there has been a loss of jobs in the traditional industries - the older service industries like the docks and the railways - and in manufacturing industries. A large number of firms have closed, many of them small firms. Sometimes this has been brought about by redevelopment, when firms have not found new premises in the area or have decided to go out of business for other reasons. Some firms have moved out of the inner city to find better sites....In some areas the main cause of job losses has been the closure of large manufacturing firms and, more generally, the shrinkage in employment in large firms.
>   There has not been enough investment in new manufacturing industry to counterbalance these job losses.

The White Paper also acknowledges that this economic attrition through mergers, rationalizations, and shift towards non-manual office work has been compounded by erratic public investment.[3]

> In some cities the processes of clearance and redevelopment have got badly out of step. The bulldozers have done their work, but the rebuilding has lagged behind. Sometimes this has been caused by changes in plans as more people left the cities than expected. In other instances it has resulted from

reductions in the allocation of resources, central and local.
Whatever the explanation, there is a wide extent of vacant
land in some inner areas, mainly in public ownership; and
there is much under-used land and property, with shops
boarded up and sites and buildings neglected.

Without effective action, the Paper admits, large numbers of
people will be left 'to face a future of declining job opportunities,
a squalid environment, deteriorating housing and declining
social services...bringing with it mounting social bitterness
and an increasing sense of alienation'.[4] The government therefore promises[5]

to give the inner areas an explicit priority in social and economic policy, even at a time of particular stringency in public resources. Comprehensive action is needed. And since
the regeneration of the inner cities will take time to achieve,
there must be a long-term commitment to tackle their problems.

The heart of the new policy is the redirection of industrial
investment: encouragement for industrial dispersion is to be
reversed, local authorities empowered and assisted to attract
firms with subsidies, loans, site preparation, buildings,
environmental improvements, and relaxed zoning.

All this acknowledges much of the analysis at which the
Community Development Project arrived. It concedes that the
behaviour of capital is crucial; that no part of the social structure can be isolated from the whole: that the quality of home
life and working life are interrelated. And if, as the Coventry
Report argued, the uncertainties of a fluctuating economy are
harshly displaced upon inner cities through the erratic adjust-
ments of public expenditure and the undetermined potential
value of their land for central city uses, as much as by the
marginality of their workers, the White Paper hints at this too -
implying by 'explicit priority' and 'long-term commitment' the
promise of a more predictable future.

So by the summer of 1977 government had redefined the ideological context of policy in terms much closer to a radical analysis. Any policy of wide enough scope to tackle structural problems must also define a field of action large enough to draw
the concerns of trade unions and community groups together,
creating a framework for the alliance of industrial and community struggles which John Benington and Jan O'Malley sought.
Conversely, in this context, explanations in terms of the social
incompetence of disadvantaged people were clearly inadequate.

The White Paper, therefore, redefined the problems so as to
open possibilities of action which had been obscured or inhibited
by community development. But at the same time it implied a
strategy whose assumptions were bound to constrain the possibilities in other ways as crucial to the coherence of policy. If

government was to manipulate the complex interaction of industrial investment, migration, housing and social services to
reverse the decline of specific inner city areas, it would have
to institute a process of planning in each of them. These plans,
if they were to represent an effective concentration of energy,
would have to define their scope in space and time. The coherence of the strategy, therefore, depended on where these
spatial and temporal boundaries were drawn. If the areas were
too large or ill-defined, the purposes and interests to be satisfied would become diffuse and amorphous; if they were too small,
they would not contain the elements of a viable social structure;
and if they were drawn in the wrong place, they would have
both these weaknesses. Similarly, if the plans were framed in
too long or short a time-span, they would not match the rate
at which changes could be made, or the need for them predicted.
However they were conceived, the boundaries would establish
a logic of proceeding which must influence action as powerfully
as the purpose of the plan itself.

These plans would also have to assume an authority to mediate between power and its use, imposing their own criteria of
relevance and coherence on the intentions of government
departments, firms, developers, public and private agencies.
Here too, if the planners mistook the limits of their authority,
they would either waste everyone's energy deciding issues over
which they had no control, and distract conflict from where the
action was, or they would take for granted what they could
question, and cramp the possibilities of planning. Hence the
way in which planners conceived of their relationship to political, economic and popular power would also largely determine
whether their work was meaningful.

The ability of comprehensive planning to reintegrate meaning
and action depends, therefore, on how these boundaries of
space, time and authority are drawn - and on whether there is
any way to draw them which makes sense. Since evasive ambiguity is the stuff of politics, policy-makers may not want to
look into these questions. But they are crucial to everyone else.
If people are to take part in planning, to treat it seriously
as a political process in which points are won or lost and collective purposes negotiated, they must first of all be satisfied
that the context of conflict and reconciliation is relevant to their
needs, and that the outcome will be decisive.

Among the first of the inner city areas chosen in the White
Paper for special attention were the surroundings of the London
docks - a five-mile stretch along both banks of the Thames of
partly abandoned docks and warehouses, declining industry,
decaying streets and raw, functional estates of public housing,
which had been designated four years earlier for comprehensive
redevelopment. Let me try to show how, in the planning of
Docklands, these questions of authority and boundary worked
themselves out. The story represents a struggle between
speculation and community, land and people, which has been

going on for nearly two hundred years, and like most of the
Docklands' history, it has moments of farce as well as bitterness,
and the drama of grandiose visions.

THE DOCKLANDS

In August 1802, the Henry Addington, guns firing and dressed
with the flags of every nation, was towed into London's first
commercial dock, under the eyes of her namesake, the prime
minister, and a crowd of spectators. The Echo, bearing a cargo
of sugar, followed in her wake. The West India Dock Company
was in business.[6]
   The dock stretched over the pastures and marshes of the
Isle of Dogs, with entrances at both Blackwall and Limehouse
reaches, cutting across the top of a southerly loop in the river.
Only a narrow, rutted road through ramshackle villages connected it by land with the city. Within the next five years,
rival companies hurried to complete docks on either side of it
and across the river on the Surrey bank - the London in Limehouse, the East India in Blackwall, the Greenland, Norway,
Baltic in Rotherhithe - in an incoherent scramble for eventually
disappointing profits. The last of the early docks, St Katharine's,
by the Tower of London, was also the first to close. Both its
building and its demolition aroused more bitterness than any
other. To dig it out, eleven thousand people were evicted from
their houses, and an ancient religious hospital destroyed. One
hundred and fifty years later, its conversion to a complex of
hotel, offices, club houses and yacht harbour represented to
the people of London's East End the kind of economic expropriation they most feared.
   At their greatest extent, the docks of London stretched
haphazardly from St Katharine's by the Tower to the Royal
docks on Gallion's reach; and around them grew up settlements
of dock and transport workers, labourers and craftsmen in the
industrial and warehousing trades attracted to the hinterland
of the port. The dock companies were never very profitable for
long, and in every crisis they turned to economies of labour -
cutting wages, putting permanent men out to casual work, hiring
by the hour only. In the 1880s a man might walk forty miles a
day for twopence, and even employers conceded that if dockers
would not work late into the afternoon, it was often from sheer
hunger. But this exploitation also provoked a tradition of
sophisticated, organized struggle. Throughout the first great
dockers' strike of 1889, a great company of 'stevedores, lighter-
men, ship-painters, sailors and firemen, riggers, scrapers,
engineers, shipwrights, permanent men[7] and casual dock
labourers, coal heavers and watermen in the scarlet coats and
pink stockings of their traditional livery, marched every mid-
day through the City of London, bands playing and banners
flying. Behind the pageantry lay a picketing organization of

military efficiency and a fund-raising drive that sustained
the strike to victory. Thirty years later, Ernest Bevin, representing the dockers before a court of inquiry into work and
wages, argued their case with the same dramatic flair. Expert
witness for the employers had claimed that a docker could
sustain a family of five on three pounds, seventeen shillings
a week. Bevin bought and prepared a meal with the exact sum
calculated in this estimate.[8]

> The next morning, Bevin asked leave to put ten plates
> before the court as evidence. The first five each contained
> a tiny portion of cabbage, potatoes and meat, the second
> equally small portions of bread and cheese. 'I ask the
> Court, my Lord,' he said 'to examine the dinner which
> Counsel for the Employers considers adequate to sustain
> the strength of a docker hauling seventy-one tons of wheat
> a day on his back.'

Bevin won his case. But as so often in the history of the
docks, organization and advocacy could not sustain victory
against the underlying weakness of unskilled labour in a system
of casual working. From the outset, London's docks had been
haphazardly laid out, quickly outdated, and mutually frustrating in their competition. They kept in business partly because
the Port of London, however inefficient, was the capital of an
empire; but even more because whenever their commercial
survival was threatened, they relentlessly drove down the price
of labour. The merging of the dock companies into a public
authority at the beginning of this century did not fundamentally
change this balance of militancy and vulnerability. When the
dockers at last gained security after the Second World War,
their way of life and the communities they had made, with all
their pride of craft, and practical radicalism, grimness and
history, were already facing drastic transformation. The old
docks, trapped by the congested city which had grown up
around them, were not adaptable to the intensive mechanization
which would keep them profitable. The work had long been
edging down river to Tilbury. In the 1960s, the Port of London
Authority staked its future on the modernization of a new
container port there, and began to see its old docks as valuable
disposable real estate, by which to finance ambitious facilities
for super-tankers even further out on the Essex marshes.
St Katherine's, the London and Surrey docks were all closed
by the end of 1970, the West India and Millwall virtually abandoned seven years later. Meanwhile, mechanization and rationalization halved the labour force. There had been 52,000
registered dockers in 1920, in 1969 there were still 23,000.
Four years later 12,000 remained and the Port of London
Authority itself, in its whole system, employed only seven and
a half thousand people.[9]

The same pressures were forcing all the traditional industries

of Docklands to close or abandon the congested and obsolete
infrastructure for cheaper and more accessible sites elsewhere.
Jobs were disappearing faster than people. Between 1961 and
1971, the boroughs of east and south-east London along the
river lost nearly 117,000 jobs in transport and manufacture,
and gained less than a fifth as many in other work.[10] In the
next three years, the rate of jobs lost in industry and transport rose from 3 to 5 per cent a year, six times as fast as for
the country as a whole. Unemployment for men in the heart of
Docklands was triple the national average, and incomes were
falling. Migration threatened to leave the poorest and least
skilled behind in a spreading wasteland of industrial decline,
surrounded by a city and region still the most prosperous in
Britain. The Docklands were plunged into a crisis of structural
adaptation more suddenly than anyone had foreseen.[11] Its
people no longer confronted the harsh poverty of industrial
exploitation, but they feared another kind of exploitation: the
appropriation of their neighbourhoods for office developments,
fashionable riverside hotels and apartments, trunk roads and
yacht harbours, for the benefit of outsiders.

'THE GREATEST CHALLENGE OF OUR TIME'

If the decline of the docks was a crisis to the people who lived
beside them, it was also to others a dramatic opportunity. Five
thousand acres of obsolete docks, warehouses and a huge
gasworks made redundant by piped natural gas, interspersed
with enclaves of shabby terraced cottages and public housing,
lay open for redevelopment in the heart of the capital. 'All the
essential ingredients are present for something "big" to happen
here,' observed Peter Walker, the Conservative government's
Secretary for the Environment, when he announced a planning
study in 1970.[12] Several sites were close enough to the financial
heart of the capital to attract ambitious office development;
St Katherine's Dock was already being transformed into a
complex of offices, hotel, yacht harbour and luxury apartments;
warehouses were being converted for adventurous professional
households along the river; and some of the old-established
wharfing companies were turning into property developers,
promoting schemes for expensive apartments along their quays.
The Minister for the Environment, Peter Walker, himself co-
founder of an aggressive investment company with property
interests, saw an extraordinary chance to transform the commercial riverside into a city within the city, where private
capital and public planning would create an altogether new
balance of social classes, amenities and economic functions,
revitalizing London as a whole. The congested roads to the East
could be widened and re-aligned, a new artery cut through to
the south-east; the river prospect opened up by parks with
boating, harbours, golf courses, pleasure gardens. The

possibilities seemed unbounded. No other great city had such
a chance within its grasp - 'the largest single area of urban
redevelopment in Europe today, and the largest that has arisen
in London since the Great Fire of 1666', four fifths of it already
owned by public bodies. In the words of a government White
Paper, 'The redevelopment of the London Docklands is, of its
kind, the greatest challenge of our time.'[13]

But this dramatization of opportunity rested on a very arbitrary conception. Only by drawing an irregular line eastwards
along both banks of the river, swerving to avoid every built
up area, could the declining docks, the marshes and redundant
gasworks be isolated from their hinterland as a continuous par-
cel of largely unpopulated and unused land. This 'Docklands'
did not correspond to any local government boundary, economic
interrelationship or traffic pattern, nor to any recognized sense
of place. The inhabitants thought of themselves as living in
Rotherhithe, Wapping, Silvertown, Isle of Dogs - distinct
parishes with their own particular qualities, isolated from each
other by the winding river.

Correspondingly, the notion of a vast acreage of available
urban land rested on a distant vision, rather than present
opportunity: many of the docks were still in use, and the Port
of London Authority had not made up its mind when or if to
abandon them; the Gas Corporation wanted to maintain its
huge, idle works, as a resource which might be needed again
when natural gas ran out. Only by drawing the spatial and
temporal boundaries very differently from the way in which
people experienced them and were used to thinking of them,
could the sense of a unique, dramatic opportunity be sustained.

The boroughs of Tower Hamlets, Southwark, Greenwich,
Lewisham and Newham saw the opportunities and problems
created by the decline of the docks as part of the needs of
each borough as a whole, relating the docks to their hinterland
rather than to other docks down or across the river. Many of
the borough councillors mistrusted the conception of Docklands,
as a device by a Conservative government to take control of
developable sites out of the hands of securely Labour councils.
The Trades Union Congress, at the first conferences it had
ever held on urban planning issues, explicitly rejected it as
undermining working-class interests. By proposing a plan for
Docklands, Peter Walker created a context which was itself
controversial.

Once the issue of redevelopment was raised, it brought out
conflicts of local against regional control, of working class
against middle class, of capital against labour. The Conservative government wanted to open the way for private capital to
revitalize eastern London, transforming the social structure,
so that the children and grandchildren of dockers might eventually find their place as workers in a predominantly commercial,
financial and service economy. The Greater London Council was

eager for land to rehouse people from all over London, and
to restore a workable balance of population, open space, public
and private housing between the inner and outer boroughs.
The outer boroughs themselves represented predominantly
middle-class interests, and saw in Docklands an opportunity
both to deflect pressure on them for public housing and to
relieve commuter traffic along new arterial roads and river-
crossings. Conversely, the boroughs along the commercial
river desperately needed sites to house their own constituents,
fearing that the younger, most skilled workers, unable to
rent or buy decent homes they could afford, would abandon
the East End, compounding its economic decline. The people
in Docklands saw themselves threatened by office developers,
by an invasion of homeless families herded into huge, impersonal
Greater London Council estates; by the conversion of the riverside into fashionable, luxury hotels and apartments; and by
main roads slashing through what was left of their disintegrating, blighted and economically marginal communities. These
far-reaching conflicts of interest and perception were crucial,
and the replanning of Docklands would only be meaningful if
it succeeded in articulating them.

THE PROMISE OF PLANNING

From every point of view, planning had risks; but without it,
the pervasive uncertainty would impoverish all the possibilities
of development. Each interest confronted planning ambivalently,
as both a threat and a promise. For those who lived in Docklands, the spatial boundaries of the plan could be used to dilute
their claims, isolating the abandoned docks from their hinterland to create a resource for London as a whole. The plan could
then rationalize wholesale expropriation, and if it was prepared
with an appearance of public consultation, it would even seem
to have the consent of its victims. Yet without a plan, the docks
would be appropriated piecemeal, mostly for office blocks and
public housing, through a series of bargains between local
councils and property developers, where the council would try
to exact as much gain in public housing and revenue as it could
in return for planning permission. Piecemeal development was
unlikely to protect local interests effectively; it fragmented
protest in campaigns against specific negotiations which were
hard to follow or understand, and scarcely open to public
intervention; and the East End boroughs lacked the planning
staff and financial sophistication to bargain forcefully against
property companies, which could set more staff on a single
project than the councils had available for the whole borough.
Nor could such development provide a context in which the
future for the people of the area could be comprehensively
tackled. If, too, their needs could only be met by regenerating
a manufacturing economy, the national government would have

to change its regional policies, provide subsidies and public capital; and it was unlikely to do this except in response to a strategic plan which it had itself promoted. So although a comprehensive plan for Docklands put the interests of its present inhabitants at risk, they would be in an even weaker position to defend them without it.

Correspondingly, developers risked frustrating delays and a more articulate opposition if the area was subjected to thorough, open planning, in which the public was consulted. But without a plan, they would have to commit themselves to negotiations where widespread local resentment might be reflected in disconcerting changes in council policy, and where the future economy and social structure would be harder to predict. In these circumstances, they were likely to take fewer risks, investing only where they could realize the quickest and most assured profits, and driving harder bargains. They would concentrate on sites which could be exploited as a peripheral extension of the financial heart of London. Even from their own point of view, office space at the margin between the city and a decaying East End was a more vulnerable investment than if it could be integrated with a comprehensive redevelopment.

In principle, therefore, everyone stood to gain from planning. It could never reconcile the underlying conflicts of interest. But only an intelligent co-ordination of uses, resourceful enough to reverse a progressive structural disintegration, was likely to sustain the value of any particular use. A planned compromise between competing needs could have more vitality, more meaning, than an unplanned, incremental disposal of particular sites, from every point of view - given that the area was not generally attractive enough to private investment except in the context of complementary public investment, and public investment could not disregard the interests of the people who lived in Docklands.

Yet planning is a political act, and no invitation to take part in it is disinterested. Peter Walker clearly had something in mind which East Enders might well distrust. To engage in planning on someone else's terms, you have to give up the autonomy of your purposes and understanding, forced to interpret them in a context of meaning which you do not altogether share. The process of reconciling conflicting needs and definitions of the issues creates its own structure of meaning, which does not correspond to the way in which any of the participants would prefer to interpret the realities of their situation. Hence, only for the planners, who are professionally committed to the process, does the meaning lie within the plan itself: for everyone else, planning is a political means from which they will be tempted to withdraw, covertly or openly, whenever there is a better way of pursuing their advantage.

Even if the alternative to negotiation can only be more damaging to your interests, there is a cost to compromising the integrity of your purpose. You become an accomplice in qualifying your own claims, in acknowledging the rationality of partial disappointment: and this can be harder to assimilate than externally imposed defeat. A group may be demoralized, its leadership discredited, by a compromise which is none the less reasonable. Hence the refusal to compromise can be a necessary strategy of self-preservation, because it preserves the integrity of purpose and understanding. Keeping faith may matter more than the expediency of the outcome.

So although everyone could see that only an intelligent, sustained plan of action could hope to rescue Docklands from an incoherent, mutually frustrating and abortive exploitation of its opportunities, no one was therefore unreservedly committed to finding such a plan. If people were alienated by assumptions that they could not challenge, they would opt out, try other means to get what they wanted, and repudiate responsibility for the outcome as a whole. Planned change, as a mutually responsive process of intelligent adaptation, could easily be overwhelmed by a much cruder and less resourceful political allocation. It depended on sustaining a framework of negotiation in which each crucial interest could continually test the tentative formulations of the plan against its purposes, so that no discussion was foreclosed, no decision pre-empted, before the meaning of agreement had been fully assimilated and accepted. Planning would have to articulate a subtle, self-reflective process of collective learning, through which to explore what sense the possible forms of co-operative adaption might make from each point of view - evolving a mutual understanding of the needs, the structural problems, the power to act. It was therefore an extraordinarily precarious and difficult endeavour, where there could be no final reconciliation - only a mutual recognition that some planned resolutions would work better for everyone than none at all.

THE FIRST PLANNING EXERCISE

As it happened, the first exercise in the replanning of Dockland was so wholly insensitive to these issues that it served, paradoxically, to make everyone more aware of them by its clumsiness. The Conservative government and the Greater London Council hired a firm of consulting engineers to draw up a series of options for the eventual future of Docklands, as a basis of public discussion and choice. The terms of reference reflected Peter Walker's vision of a five and a half thousand acre vacant lot, straddling the banks of the commercial river, whose potential use, twenty years on, would be virtually unconstrained by its past. Handed such a blank sheet, the consultants proceeded by permuting and combining the possible patterns of land use as they might appear in 1990. About thirty such designs evolved, mixing public and private housing, offices, factories, parks in every conceivable proportion, with

more adventurous proposals – a monorail, yacht harbour, fun-
fair or safari park – enhancing somewhat randomly one conception or another. To each was attached an evocative label 'East
End Consolidated' (a mass of public housing); 'Europa' (mostly
offices for international companies and agencies); 'Fun City'
(emphasizing playgrounds); 'Venice' (emphasizing yacht harbours). The more fanciful of these possibilities were eliminated
and the rest reduced to five ('Waterside', 'Thames Park', 'East
End Consolidated', 'Europa' and 'City New Town') which were
then presented to the boroughs and the residents of Docklands
by a report,[14] pamphlets, and exhibitions. Social surveys and
questionnaires placed at the exhibitions were designed to elicit
popular preferences. But most people were bemused by the
brightly coloured mosaics which mapped these remote, notional
futures. Embarrassed planners tried to interest East Enders
in visions of lions or golfers roaming across the Isle of Dogs,
or lectured on advanced transport technology near closed
underground stations and people sleeping in the street. 'It
was a load of old balls,' remarked one resident who had attended
such meetings.[15]

Where was there room for a golf course on the Isle of Dogs?
People fell about laughing. Then the speaker began talking
about this new railway that runs on rubber wheels, and
how it could climb much steeper gradients than an ordinary
train. He got out diagrams and was going on about it when
someone asked, where is there a hill between Tilbury and
Tower Bridge? It was a load of codswallop. It's very difficult in an area like this to talk in the abstract – you need
to talk about widening West Ferry Road. Planning is really
about your street, your area – and widening people's hori-
zons, showing the implications of something like a shopping
centre. And these exhibitions, where you walk in and are
given a piece of paper to put your views are no good. I
defy even an architect in five minutes and ten words to make
a detailed criticism. People just mention this or that which
occurs to them at the moment – like they want open space,
or a shopping centre. Afterwards they may go home and
have second thoughts, but they can't change what they've
written, they can only go and fill in another slip of paper –
so what they said first still stands.

Although 350,000 leaflets, and 70,000 shortened versions of
the consultants' report were distributed, one hundred illustrated
talks given, seven information centres opened for three months
– at a cost of about eighty thousand pounds – only twelve
hundred comments were received from the public. Some meetings attracted no audience at all, attendance at the Information
Centres averaged a hundred a week, and of those who accepted
a questionnaire, only one in ten bothered to return it. As the
leader of the Docklands planning team admitted, 'It is doubtful

whether even in the most favourable circumstances the presen-
tation of five consultants' options ever stood a fair chance of
being accepted by the public as an impartial and receptive
approach.[16] Several of the five Docklands boroughs were
equally critical of so arbitrary and superficial a forcing of
choice. With a change of government both nationally and in the
Greater London Council, the whole exercise was set aside, and
the process of planning started afresh.

THE SECOND PLANNING EXERCISE

A new structure evolved, with a planning team responsible to
the Greater London Council and the five boroughs in which
Docklands lies, and an advisory council on which local groups
were represented. This advisory council invited representatives
from the Trades Union Congress, the local trades councils,
tenants' associations, local societies, churches and colleges,
and the Canning Town Community Development Project to meet
periodically to review the discussion papers prepared by the
planning team, and put forward ideas of their own. By this
time, residents, alerted to the issues, had set up their own
organizations, recruiting professional help; these action groups
were recognized and incorporated in the advisory council. But
the new consultative structure scarcely worked any better than
the old. The hope of a genuinely participatory process was
foredoomed by the underlying spatial definition of the task. If
you draw a boundary round five and a half thousand acres and
call for a plan of its future, how else are planners to proceed
except by a sequential logic of design - first establishing the
general principles of the whole and then, step by step, setting
out their implications in increasingly predetermined forms? The
physical frame imposes a hierarchy of decisions, from those
which shape the picture as a whole, to those which render its
details; and once a higher order decision has been taken, it
cannot be reversed without unravelling months or years of
work. Unless public participation corresponds to this sequence
and respects it, its intervention becomes endlessly disruptive.
  Thus the planning team resisted any independent initiative
from local residents, protesting against 'a participation exercise
which would militate against observing the tight timetable...
agreed for the preparation of the main strategy'.[17] In general,
while the public should be informed and sometimes consulted
about each stage in the development of the plan, the officials
maintained that residents could practicably only play an active
part in detailed, local design - when the 'commanding factors'
determining the plan had already become 'fixed points in public
discussion'.[18] This policy made mutual frustration inevitable.
For if crucial decisions were taken over residents' heads, when
the implications became evident in the rebuilding of their immediate surroundings they were bound to revive all the issues

which the planners would wish to take as settled. To the people
of Docklands the separation between strategic choice and con-
sequent implementation was meaningless, because they could
only test the strategy by what it did for them in their particular
living space. If they were to have any control over what happened, they had to reject the logic which seemed to the planners a prerequisite of rational decision.

But any coherent opposition to this logic was very difficult
to articulate. The neighbourhoods around each dock had been
used to struggling in isolation against neglect and decay, preoccupied with particular campaigns – in Wapping, for instance,
against the encroachment of the St Katherine's development;
in the Isle of Dogs for a school, a better bus service; and,
though they were less than a mile apart, the river separated
and distinguished them. In each neighbourhood, therefore,
those who read the consultants' report tended to see in it, at
first, the embodiment of the local threat they most feared –
expropriation by office development, or a motorway, the abandonment of the surviving docks, the gentrification of the riverside. The energy, leadership and popular support for organization in response to the plans arose, at least on the north bank
of the Thames, from previous local campaigns of protest. But
opposition alone was a lost cause: without planning, all the
neighbourhoods were doomed to disintegration. In rejecting
the consultants' report, and the constricted opportunity for
public participation proposed in the structure which succeeded
it, the organizations of protest had also, in their own interests,
to put forward an alternative conception of planning to which
they could all agree.

THE ACTION GROUPS

Four loosely organized, informal action groups evolved – for the
East End, the Isle of Dogs, and the Surrey Docks; and a Joint
Docklands Action Group designed to co-ordinate their response
to the formal planning structure as a whole. Each represented
a small network of people in community affairs – councillors
and council candidates, social workers, a settlement house
warden, the leader of a tenant's association, representatives
of trades councils, college teachers – who either worked or
lived in the neighbourhood. Meetings might attract ten or
twenty, but the core of each group consisted of no more than
half a dozen: and within the group, a professionally trained
planner or community worker was the sustaining organizer. The
Joint Dockland Action Group, especially, was not a community
organization but a steering committee of representatives from
the other groups, through which to endorse a continuous critique of the documents, proposals and actions coming from the
planning team, the boroughs and the Port of London Authority.
At the outset, it depended greatly on the skill and determination

of Rhoda Brawne, an American planner, trained at the Massachusetts Institute of Technology, who worked formally for a family advice centre in the East End. She wrote incisive papers for both the Action Groups and the Tower Hamlets Council, criticizing plans, arguing for more representative procedures, proposing alternatives, initiating legal action against the Port Authority for filling docks without planning permission. But this sophisticated advocacy was inevitably drawn into the context of a debate with the official planning team, two steps removed from popular feeling. The three local action groups were not consistently involved in it, seeing it as somewhat remote from their immediate concerns; and they themselves were often working to evoke public interest rather than react to particular proposals. The action groups owed their vitality mostly to local political leaders, professional planners and community organizers, who understood how to relate the implications of strategic planning to their sense of what the people of Docklands most wanted, and could use their community networks to call meetings and mobilize protest. Correspondingly, the Joint Docklands Action Group, especially, became valuable to the planning team, as an articulate representation of local feeling with whom to debate and negotiate issues in terms the planners acknowledged. The action groups were invited on to the advisory council, and the Joint Action Group received increasing government money for a small professional staff.

The action groups were only one expression of several related campaigns. The men and women most involved in them were also active in the local Labour Party, the trades councils, tenants' associations and community affairs. The East End had a long tradition of organized political protest. There had been a stubborn strike against the Conservative government's policy of economic rents in public housing; a few years earlier, the Isle of Dogs had declared its independence of the United Kingdom, barricading the only two roads into the peninsular, in protest against the closing of a school and neglect of its needs. The local councillors themselves were often sympathetic: the leader of the Tower Hamlets Council had won his position by his stand against a property development his predecessor had been negotiating. If the action groups could influence plans, it was largely because established political organizations were fighting the same battle.

Nor was the plan itself the only issue, or even the most obviously important issue, to tackle. Campaigns to prevent disruptive road-widening schemes or building over open space, to get a new school or stop docks closing seemed more urgent. The Joint Docklands Action Group was as much concerned with pressing the Port of London Authority not to close the Millwall Dock as with criticizing planning proposals.

But if planning, and the action groups' reponse to it, were often marginal to a much more complex process of political negotiation, they dealt with issues which other campaigns did

not confront. Struggles over docks, roads, schools or housing
were worthwhile only if the communities had a future; and
planning, more than these other campaigns, represented a
commitment to defining and creating that future.

The experience of the Community Development Projects
showed that the issue for inner city neighbourhoods was not
only the distribution of resources, within an institutional structure of allocation grudgingly open to community pressure, but
the distribution of uncertainty, in a society with a precarious
economic future, growing ideological self-doubt, and declining
public resources. Although the people who lived by the docks
had protested vigorously against higher rents, lack of schools,
public transport, and open space, and won concessions, none
of this helped to resolve the uncertainty of their future. Unless
schools, housing, jobs, services were related in some sustain-
able pattern, the concessions meant very little. Hence the
people of Docklands needed, above all, a commitment to some
conception of their future which would not be continually undermined by erratic, short-sighted accommodation to economic
events. Government, too, needed such a conception, if it was
to reverse an alarming decay of inner London. In these circumstances, planning represented not only a means of determining
who would get how much of what, but a promise that a demoralizing concentration of uncertainty would be deflected from the
inner cities. If government, as the White Paper announced,
was prepared to give priority to the inner cities - to sustain
a far-sighted strategy despite the precariousness of the national
economy, and to recognize that the first need was to recreate
stable jobs for the people who lived there - then the people
who lived by the docks had most to gain by holding government
to its promise.

Plans are designed to create predictable, orderly relationships,
and so to establish control. The power to make and carry out
plans is therefore the power to control, and it is easy to conclude from this that planning merely rationalizes and secures
the structure of power whenever it is threatened. In these
terms, to be sure, the less your stake in that structure, the
less you have to gain from any part in planning: you can only
hope to exact a higher price for being controlled. But the victims of urban disintegration are not so much controlled as
discarded, the wasted assets abandoned by economic dislocation.
They suffer most of all from the lack of any predictable, orderly
relationships through which to establish a sense of their future.
In these terms, the failure to plan for them at all is a more
fundamental measure of their victimization than the constraints
which planning imposes.

The Docklands communities therefore had to balance the need
for planning against their mistrust of the spatial and political
framework within which it had been set. The action groups
were continually tempted to withdraw from the advisory council
and repudiate responsibility for negotiating an acceptable docu-

ment; and yet in the end they persisted, patiently, in a long drawn-out critical review of the position papers produced by the planning team. The Docklands Strategic Plan, published in July 1976, shows the influence of this critique.

THE STRATEGIC PLAN

In the first place, the plan is not now presented as a vast, public real estate development, but as a set of principles, derived from an analysis of underlying social and economic decline, whose spatial and temporal reference is no longer arbitrarily bounded.[19]

Docklands is an inseparable part of the urban areas surrounding it. The social, economic and environmental problems of Docklands are in all respects part of the same problems affecting a wider area of East London. To talk solely of the social and economic state of Docklands as though these issues were confined within a line on a map would be artificial and would disguise the fundamental nature of some of the issues.

The plan recognizes, too, that the control of uncertainty, and uncertainty of control are inseparable:[20]

Uncertainty about the future is a major factor like land, population and finance to be taken into account when planning. The essential purpose of a plan for a complex activity such as Docklands, where many different people and agencies are involved and where anything one does depends upon others, is to reduce the uncertainty about what other people are going to do and ensure as far as possible that individual actions and decisions combine to achieve the intended objective. The plan will not do this if it is so general that 100 different people can interpret everything it says in 100 different ways. Neither will it do this if it is based on the illusion that all future influences are known, for events will expose the illusion and the plan will lack credibility.

Thus Docklands is no longer seen as a place, but a 'complex activity', reaching out indeterminately in space and time – adapting, learning, but always guided by an evolving structure of purpose. Within this conceptual framework, the plan presents the future of industrial employment as the crucial problem:[21]

If the current rate of decline in manufacturing jobs were to continue, then there would be insufficient jobs available in East London to cater for the needs of the resident population, even if the latter were to continue to decline as in the

past. If it were possible to make up this deficiency by providing more jobs in services which have been growing, the
structure of employment would change radically from 29
per cent manufacturing, 35 per cent services in 1971 to 11
per cent manufacturing, 50 per cent services in 1981. This
would mean an enormous switch in aptitudes and skills of
the resident work force in ten years. Far more than could
be expected from the natural change due to recruitment
and retirement....The capacity of the area to continue to
absorb this rate of fundamental change without very severe
social upheaval must be in doubt, even if it were thought
desirable.

And the authors of the plan do not believe that office-based
services can or should - for the health of the national economy
- grow at such an overwhelming rate.
      The strategy, then, is to hold back the decline of manufac-
ture and stabilize it, by every means available: but especially
by manipulating the two factors most within the control of
planning - public housing and transport policy. New roads and
an underground line are to link the neighbourhoods of Docklands, east and west. New houses, attractive to skilled workers
- which, perhaps, they might own or partly own - are to draw
them back, hold them, and release land elsewhere in the East
End for industrial growth. Land is to be reserved for the full
range of community and welfare services, of shopping and open
space, to ensure for the people who live around the docks a
range of amenities comparable to other, more fortunate, London-
ers, while respecting their style of life. And all these actions
are to be concerted: industrial promotion without better transportation and housing, housing without services and amenities,
will all fail. 'Only if the strategy is seen to be a radical, coherent and practical attempt to tackle the problems that are widely
recognized within a stated time will confidence be rekindled.'[22]
      The Joint Docklands Action Group was sceptical of much of
this strategy. It doubted whether skilled workers needed to
be attracted back, and disliked the idea of diluting public housing with forms of home ownership which most people could not
afford. A new underground link would take a long time to
build, even if government agreed to put up the money. The
industrial strategy was weak - too dependent on unpromising
private investment. The action group urged, rather, public
investment through the National Enterprise Board, more imaginative efforts to save some of the inner London Docks, more
government subsidy. It wanted more buses, fewer disruptive
new roads. But it accepted the essential definitions of the problems, the principles and priorities of need, as the plan
presented them.[23] The strategic plan emerged as a meaningful
framework of action, within which conflicts over the practicality,
fairness and class-bias of means could be purposefully engaged.
It seemed to vindicate both the professional advocacy of the

action groups, whose insistent criticism had helped to recast
the whole approach in terms which made sense to the people
living by the docks; and the procedures of the planners, who
for all their patronizing defensiveness had in the end listened
and learned - at least when action groups and local governments
spoke with the same voice.

The first planning document, with its five choices, had tried
to make action meaningful by referring it to a finished design -
much as painting on a canvas has, as its context of meaning,
the picture it will produce. So the evolution of Docklands was
presented as stages in the painting of pictures - squares and
lines of symbolic colour, which swelled and joined in an emerging pattern. This is the master builder's vision, where the
present is already history: and it exacts an extraordinary
ideological commitment. If the plans had been less mechanically
derived, if consultation had concerted them into a single grand
design, they might conceivably have inspired such a commitment
from national government, as had new towns a generation before:
and like new towns, the commanding structure to realize such
a vision was an autonomous development corporation.[24]

The second Strategic Plan developed a fundamentally different
structure of meaning, in which the future was acknowledged
to be unknowable. It attempted to reduce uncertainty, not by
a vision of where we were going, but by a sense of where we
were coming from. The future then became a set of trends and
consequences extrapolated from the past, to be changed by
present action in the light of our purposes. Hence the meaning
of action was to be experimental - evolving from a constant
interplay between intention and experience - but always coherent, because the framework of principles would continuously
assimilate and reintegrate them. 'This document is therefore
the starting point of a continuous evolutionary process which
can ensure that at any time there is an overall up-to-date plan
in existence capable of giving useful guidance to everyone in
all agencies.'[25] In practical terms, this suggested an incremental
strategy, where each development would be coherent and useful,
irrespective of the pace and extent of those which were to
follow.

THE WEAKNESS OF PLANNING

If the original plans were like sketches for pictures, the strategic plan was more like a programme of scientific research - a
framework of conceptions and their relationships which defined
both the significant problems and the approach to their resolution. But only scientists may practise science, and their education indoctrinates them with an unyielding loyalty to the finding
and consolidating of such a framework. Planners do not characteristically carry out their plans: and only for them is the
integrity of the framework for prospective action a constant,

crucial preoccupation. Everyone else only looks for a plan when
they are bewildered or frustrated; planning, for them, is an
episodic response to the disintegration of purpose in action.
So although the councillors of the five Docklands boroughs,
and many of the people who lived, worked, or made their money
by the docks, might agree with the need for a strategic plan,
accept its analysis and principles, they would not necessarily
protect its integrity once the conceptual crisis had been overcome. The power of the planners lay only in their ability to
resolve this crisis through their professional method. They
lacked either the moral or political authority to protect the
integrity of their conception once it was approved: and because
they foresaw an adaptive strategy of solving needs as they
evolved, they could not appeal to the commanding vision of a
final creation.

Yet, perversely, the very creation of a plan, the sense that
a framework for concerting purposeful action had been arrived
at, made short-sighted and opportunistic actions seem less
dangerous. If planners, like a priesthood, carry the ideological
burden of making sense of actions, as a social whole, then they
release everyone else from that responsibility - without even
the terror of damnation to hold against transgressors. Planners
have often been accused of rationalizing the interests of the
powerful: but it seems to me that, more characteristically, they
legitimize power by integrating its interests in a much wider
context of meaning. The problem, then, is not so much that the
meaning itself is corrupt, as that its implications are then
ignored.

This weakness of planning, as a strategy of action, was
apparent even before the plan was published. In 1974, for
instance, Trammel Crow, a Texas company, proposed to build
an international merchandise market and exhibition centre cover-
ing twenty-five acres of the abandoned Surrey Docks. The
scheme was open to a great many objections: it would have
blocked access to the river with a huge, blank, unsightly
structure; overwhelmed the surviving residential neighbourhoods with hotels, parking, amenities for commercial visitors;
imposed a public cost, originally estimated at thirty million
pounds, to widen and improve its congested roads; and provided in return few jobs or amenities for local people. The
planning team saw a much more appropriate site north of the
river.[26] The Southwark Trades Council protested that, of the
12,000 jobs it promised, only 2,000 would be open to East
Enders - fewer than from present uses - and these the most
menial. The Surrey Docks Action Group, after a change of
leadership, voted against it. Lewisham, the adjoining borough,
foresaw that it would generate unmanageable traffic conges-
tion.[27] Above all, the proposal, if it were approved, would have
pre-empted the essential purpose of the plan - to determine
the principles of a balanced, integrated structure of activities
and uses, before any sites were commandeered.

But the Trammel Crow proposal was the only specific large
private investment in Docklands to have been put forward, and
the Southwark Council supported it eagerly for the two million
in tax rates it promised to generate. The American company,
sensing its advantage, cajoled and bullied. Three planeloads
of councillors and local leaders of opinion were invited to Dallas
for a round of inspections and barbecues at Crow's palatial
home, with its impressive art collection. Fears of the company's
notoriously anti-union traditions were soothed with the offer,
not only to work with organized labour, but to provide the
Transport and General Workers' Union with an office. At the
same time, Trammel Crow threatened to withdraw unless their
proposal was approved by the end of the year without further
public inquiry.

Under this pressure, the commitment to planning collapsed.
The five boroughs and the Greater London Council, who con-
stituted the Joint Docklands Committee, seem to have agreed
that Southwark could have the trade mart it wanted, so long
as the other boroughs could each claim the same undisputed
indulgence of their own favourite projects. The Greater London
Council formally approved the scheme in April 1975. The Secretary for the Environment, of the national government was
equally reluctant to harass the proposers of so large an investment. The planning team obediently reworked their estimates
of the public costs in road improvement and infrastructure,
from thirty million to nine.[28] So over the next year the trade
mart was rationalized and accommodated into the Strategic Plan,
as a point of reference for the redevelopment of the whole of
Surrey Docks.

Three months after the plan was published, Trammel Crow
announced that they were postponing the project indefinitely,
until there was a significant improvement in the general investment climate and a substantial fall in the level of interest
rates.[29] So, for lack of resources and political faith, planning
did not after all influence who was left to cope with the hardships of uncertainty. Trammel Crow exacted a commitment to
the company's timetable, the company's requirements, without
compromising its own freedom of manoeuvre.

Even if Trammel Crow had pursued their proposal, and
accepted the many conditions which the governing authorities
imposed, it could not easily have been held to its contract
once it had the site. The redevelopment of St Katherine's Dock
had already become imbroiled in controversy, as its builders
constantly revamped their undertaking. As originally approved,
the scheme was to provide a hotel, public and private housing,
a yacht harbour, and an exhibition centre reconstructed from
three historic warehouses designed by Thomas Telford early in
the last century. It soon appeared that the Greater London
Council and the company, Taylor Woodrow, had different ideas
of what an exhibition centre meant. The council, understandably, foresaw an exhibition space, exploiting the handsome

industrial architecture; but Taylor Woodrow had from the first
intended to build mostly exclusive office accommodation for the
executives of firms with international connections, and soon
renamed the project, ambiguously, a World Trade Centre.
('We always made the office content clear,' one of their officers
protested to me. 'It's not our fault if the GLC misunderstood.'[130])
The planning authorities protested against this redefinition,
but while the project was stalled in controversy one of the
warehouses was burned down by arson and the company eventually negotiated permission to destroy the third 'C' warehouse,
so long as it used the materials to rebuild the second, 'B' warehouse. Taylor Woodrow had originally described its intentions
for the 'B' warehouse, in these terms:[31]

> This building runs the whole length of the West Quay pro-
> viding splendid vistas. The recent unsightly concrete
> columns will be removed. Glass walls inside the columns
> will enclose the space which will be used for exhibition
> purposes. The splendid porte cochere will become an
> entrance hall. In the North Pavilion of 'B' part of the mez-
> zanine from 'C' warehouse will be incorporated when it will
> form a working section of the warehouse complete with
> hydraulic winches and jigger. This will be an authentic
> architectural and archaeological microcosm of the Telford/
> Hardwich design.

But no sooner was this agreed than the company launched a
campaign for the destruction of the 'B' warehouse, too, as an
anachronistic 'brontosaurus' - citing Mao Tse Tung and the
Moscow World Trades Centre to convince its critics that such
historic preservation was out of keeping with the spirit of the
times.[32] Meanwhile, the company made a variety of detailed
revisions in its plans, which the public authorities had little
choice but to ratify after the fact. These cumulative changes
led towards a complex of hotel and office accommodation, insulated from the surrounding neighbourhood by further demolition and eviction, in which the provision of housing for local
people became vestigial. However the council and the local
residents might protest, however they felt they had been taken
in, in the last resort what could they do? The development was
in Taylor Woodrow's hands, and no one else had the resources,
even if they could claim the right, to take it from them. For its
part, the company insisted that it was only trying to retrieve a
modest profit from a public-spirited, costly and financially
doubtful enterprise.

Such projects are the cuckoos' eggs of planning. Planners
hatch them, nurture them, feed their growing appetites only
to have them toss from the nest the planners own fledglings -
the low-cost housing, civic amenities, historic buildings. Planning, on the scale of Docklands, has such weak control, because
its authority is essentially a structure of permissions. Once it

is no longer concerned with single, immediate projects, but a complex of developments extending into an indeterminate future, it becomes a set of principles designed to guide, co-ordinate and adapt decisions continuously in the light of events; a frame of reference for the experience and purposes of all the actors, which arbitrates and resolves into common strategy what they have learned. But the formal power of planners is largely to recommend that permission to build be withheld or granted. The act of securing permission is only an episode in the life of a project. So long as each such grant represents a small discrete commitment of space and over time, the planners can still, in an evolving mosaic of permissions, guide and learn. But the temptation, and perhaps the need, is to anchor developments of the scale of Docklands in very large, mixed, farseeing projects: the trade mart, the St Katherine's complex of hotel, trade centre, yacht harbour, shops, public and private housing; the proposal of offices, housing, a polytechnic, school and small scale manufacturing for the East London docks. Each of these represents a political deal, where permission for profitable development is traded against private investment in public goods: office space for council housing, hotel for historic preservation, trade mart for park. The developer is taxed, formally, on his profits by the rates he pays; and by negotiation on his conception, through the land he buys but gives back for public use, the public housing he builds. But the parties to the bargain are left with very unequal powers to enforce their agreement. The developer controls the land and the resources; the public authority cannot revoke its permission, because it has very little choice but to see whatever has been started through, on whatever terms private capital will accept, since it lacks resources of its own. Its only sanction is to impose delays, by calling the developer to account - and that cuts both ways. So while the Docklands team conceived of planning as continuous guidance and learning, its powers were largely concentrated in recommending discontinuous acts of permission.

Unreserved honesty in negotiation, and scrupulous faithfulness to the spirit of an agreement, are not, perhaps, the best prescription for profitable building. But even the most honourable developer is bound by the market: if interest rates go up, the demand for office space goes down, costs or wages rise, there are any number of excuses for revising the scheme. The developer's own interests have intersected with the planners' design only at one crucial moment of time: thereafter the context of action remains, as it has always been, the market. Neither the planners nor the authorities for which they work can do much to influence that market.

This disparity between the context of planning and the context of action was even harder to bridge in drawing to the Dockland neighbourhoods the industry in which their future was to be grounded. Paper after paper - from the planning

team, the boroughs, the Docklands action groups and local
trades councils, the Trades Union Congress - reiterated the
same bleak analysis. The profitability and international competitiveness of British manufacture had been steadily declining;
closures, rationalizations and more automated production had,
in the past fifteen years, reduced manufacturing employment
in the nation by 9 per cent; and in London, with its smaller,
older, more labour-intensive plants, skilled and organized
workforce, and costly, sometimes congested sites, employment
had fallen by 34 per cent. Meanwhile, jobs in financial, professional, administrative, transport and storage business had
risen rapidly - but these did not compensate in numbers for
the losses in manufacture, they were not for the most part suit-
able for the manual workers of the East End, and such manual
work as they offered was at a lower wage than industry. At the
same time, national government had for years been encouraging
the relocation of industry outside London, partly to relieve
the overcrowding of the city and establish the new towns on
its outskirts, and partly to redirect investment to the poorer
regions of the country. Hence the Dockland parishes had borne
the hardships of an economic restructuring which had worked,
and been encouraged to work, for the benefit of other settlements.

National government could - and did cautiously - begin to
revise its policy on industrial location. But without a much
larger, direct share in economic investment, the planable means
to redress the imbalance were mostly spatial - improving road
and rail access to sites, developing industrial estates and
factory space, ensuring housing to attract skilled workers -
and these improvements were marginal to the problems most
employers faced.

Sugar-refining and the manufacture of sweeteners, for
instance, employed over three thousand people in the Docklands
works of three large companies. All intended to remain, and
had invested heavily in new plant and buildings. But their
future depended on the intricate politics of the international
sugar economy. An eight-million-pound investment in a sweet-
ener derived from maize was unexpectedly undermined by a
protectionist Common Market levy; the world sugar market was
unstable; and cane refining capacity redundant, as European
governments protected their domestic beet growers. At best,
the companies might hold the loss of jobs to a gradual attrition.[33]

The clothing industry employed sixteen thousand people in
the Docklands borough of Tower Hamlets alone. But by 1970
the largest companies were increasingly shifting their production
to Turkey, Greece, North Africa and Hong Kong where labour
was cheaper; between 1971 and 1973 imported clothes on the
British market doubled. At the same time, they were relocating
their investment in home production outside London, or sub-
contracting to small firms at very low profit margins - who in
turn sub-contracted at even lower rates to homeworkers. Hence

in two years, employment had fallen by 20 per cent in parts of
the borough, and the work that remained was more and more to
be found in illegal basement sweatshops. Homeworking had
doubled, union membership fallen from ten to two thousand.
Conditions of work were becoming so unstable, exploitative and
unsafe that vacancies could no longer be filled. Yet the industry was barely profitable.[34]

In search of cheaper labour and more automated plant, a
manufacturer of telephone and cable equipment, the largest
British subsidiary of ITT, had moved some of its production
to another city, and concentrated in Docklands work which
employed mostly women.[35] Breweries had merged and closed.
Industrial sites were being turned over to lorry parking, warehousing and storage. In the face of these bleak realities, pro-
nouncements by political leaders began to sound more desperate
and fanciful. 'We will do anything to encourage, advise and
help anyone who is willing to play a part in bringing life back
to this area,' Horace Cutler, leader of the Greater London
Council, promised an audience of Dutch industrialists in Amster-
dam, as he held out prospects of a free port, exhibition and
cultural centres, new roads, new underground railways, and
'perhaps' - words hobbling after vision - 'a Euro-style Tivoli
gardens type of development'.[36]

In practice, however, government was compounding the
decline of the Docklands boroughs by the constraints of its own
economic policies. In the four years from 1974 to 1978 national
government had pressed local authorities as a whole to reduce
their capital expenditures by half. In the five boroughs expenditures on land acquisition, public housing, social services,
roads and transportation were all declining. The more ambitious
road and underground railway proposals of the Docklands plan
had been postponed ten years. To save recurrent costs,
boroughs were reducing staff, raising rents, and absolving
themselves of responsibility for decoration and minor repairs.
Just as the industrial strategy set out to create new jobs, and
ended as a rearguard against progressive decline, so the public
investment strategy set out to rebuild, and ended by taking
away with one hand what it put forward in the other.

The ambivalence of government, caught between inflation and
economic decay, undermined its promise to the inner cities of
an 'explicit priority in social and economic policy, even at a
time of particular stringency in public resources', and a 'long-
term commitment'. In effect, priority meant only that while
thirty-seven million pounds were cut from the boroughs' expenditures in 1977, seventeen million pounds were returned to them
for use in the Docklands neighbourhoods, as part of a special
inner city grant for capital works, designed to stimulate the
construction industry. But so far from contributing to the long-
term commitment, the grant was specifically to be spent by
March 1979. This constraint ruled out major work of the highest
priority, upsetting the coherence of the whole plan. For lack

of time to acquire new land, local authorities proposed that
scattered industrial sites be prepared here and there, without
the advantages of the integrated, concentrated development
the plan intended, and in one instance pre-empting land designed
for housing; some proposals lay outside Docklands altogether,
others were marginal. 'The time limit', as the director of the
Docklands Development Team pointed out, 'means that the seventeen million pounds is not necessarily the best way of launching
the project with that level of expenditure.'[37] As so often in the
history of government policy for the inner city neighbourhoods,
the promise of coherent, sustained development was once more
overwhelmed by a preoccupation with short-term national economic regulation.

To take away with one hand and give back with the other only
made sense at all so long as the issues were reduced to questions of allocating resources. Priority might then mean that,
within the context of national expenditure cuts, impoverished
city neighbourhoods were to suffer less than elsewhere; and
commitment simply that this favourable bias was to last. But the
crucial questions were not how many houses, roads or industrial
sites the boroughs might build that year. If there was no knowing when, if ever, the new underground railways would be
built; or whether demand for industrial space would conform
to the sites haphazardly preparable within a fickle budget; or
the rate at which housing projects could be sustained – then
the uncertainties of public intervention merely overlaid the
uncertainties of private investment. The people in the Docklands'
parishes would still have no future. Yet it was above all to
provide confidence in a future that the Docklands plan was
initiated. Why did government – even in the manipulation of
relationships it could directly control – undermine its own
intentions?

Planning, as a social ideal, implies a mutual exchange of
commitment to act. Most of our uncertainties concern the
behaviour of other people: hence the science and techniques
by which we try to dominate the natural world have their
counterpart in a science of human organization. And this is
what planning seeks to represent: a process of accurate des-
cription, analysis, prediction and matching of counteracting
interventions. But in a development as complex as the future
of a community or an industry, the intervening variables are
too many and too incompletely known to predict the circumstances in which these commitments must be carried out. People
try to defend themselves against commitments they may be
unable or unwilling to fulfil; and yet at the same time, the more
they can exact commitments from others, the greater the range
of relationships upon which they can rely. Command over the
future, as an ability to predict the range of possibilities, and
secure the freedom to choose the most favourable response to
each of them, becomes competitive. Everyone wants others to
be available when needed, without having to say when that will

be; wants to know the price at which he will buy, without promising the price at which to sell; wants the option, without having to take it up - just as Trammel Crow wanted an option on the Surrey Docks, without any undertaking as to when or if they would use it. Correspondingly, governments and corporations want to tell only as much about their sense of the future, and how they might respond to it, as will prepare others to do what they wish, but will not tell them what might prepare people to thwart them. So insecurity generates defences which seek competitively to transpose the burden of uncertainty on to others, undermining their ability to sustain purposes of their own.

The Docklands, as much as the neighbourhoods which concerned the Community Development Projects, suffered from an imposition of overlapping uncertainties. Most of the people who lived there had never enjoyed much economic security: dock workers had struggled free of the hardships of casual labour only to see rationalization and mechanization make most of them redundant. As economic activity declined, employment was becoming more concentrated in firms that were themselves marginal - precarious sub-contractors dependent on larger manufacturers - or cutting their workers to protect their profits. Yet at the same time, land remained costly, because so long as those who controlled it could keep open its future use, its potential value greatly exceeded its present usefulness. And these economic relationships, whereby the powerful maintained their freedom of action at the expense of those who lived in Docklands, surrounded by dilapidation that neither they nor local government had the means to redeem, and with less and less promise of reliable, worthwhile work, were overlaid by relationships of government, whereby local authority was continually constrained by national policy, but central government avoided any specific commitment of how much, or when or over how long a time, it would invest in Docklands.

Everyone, in the last resort, had to deal with the uncertainties of an international economy on which they depended, but could not control. Each firm, each level and department of government sought to maintain its freedom of manoeuvre, while binding others, in a competitive struggle to secure a predictable strategy of action. Inevitably, those who had least power to impose their purposes - owning nothing, possessing only redundant skills, unorganized, and politically discountable - bore the brunt of these uncertainties. They were not all concentrated in inner cities, but there the abandoned buildings, the vacant lots, the vandalism made evident the consequences of robbing people of a future - and this physical decay was more influential than the invisible hardships of people, undermining local government revenue, and inhibiting the realization of land values.

Government policies toward the inner city, from the Community Development Project to the redevelopment of Docklands, recog-

nized that this uncertainty was crippling. They were to find
out what help people most needed, and try to provide it; to
rescue them from a demoralizing sense of powerlessness, by
stimulating autonomous community activities; to co-ordinate
services and interventions in a coherent approach to solving
problems. Information and analysis, leading to a co-ordinated
plan of action, would restore the sense of a future. But these
ideals were unrealizable, unless the relationships which created
this crushing concentration of uncertainties were revised. In
practice, Central government gave up none of its control to
local government - committing only good intentions and sur-
rendering none of its regulative powers; the Docklands Strategic Plan had no statutory authority; and the planners refused
to be bound by what the people of the Docklands parishes
said they wanted. At the same time, government and planners
alike accepted the autonomy of economic investment - even when
they dealt with public bodies like the Port of London Authority
or the gas corporation - offering to facilitate, subsidize, advise
and accommodate, but asserting no new powers of control. So
the success of the Docklands plan rested only on the force of
a statement of intention to recreate confidence in the future:
and even before the plan was published, events showed how
readily the statement would be contradicted in the expedient
everyday exercise of power. Without deliberate or conscious
hypocrisy, government made the argument for a less demoralizing uncertainty, endorsed the strategy, but could or would
not effectively constrain the relationships responsible for creating that uncertainty. As the Docklands action groups recognized, unless government was prepared to undertake interventions 'on a scale and of a type and precision not currently
considered acceptable at a political level',[38] all their efforts to
argue the plan itself into better shape would make very little
difference.

Though the long debate between local and national governments, action groups, trade unions, planners and their consti-
tuencies had often been clumsily articulated, patronizing,
manipulative and tendentious, it had evolved a mutual understanding of the problems of the inner city and what needed to
be done. But planning, in these terms, presupposed a governmental structure capable of co-ordinating social and economic
investment. In the next few years, as the economic situation of
Britain deteriorated, the promise of redevelopment faded: funds
were cut, plans postponed, and very little of the planned investment in industry or private housing, education or public transport took place.[39] The future of the Docklands plan became
absorbed in a much broader question of whether government
still possessed the power to reconcile social needs with the pressures of economic changes.

4 EMPLOYMENT, INFLATION AND TAXES

The Community Development Project, the Inner City Studies, the Docklands plan had all come to much the same conclusions about the causes of inner city decline, and the kinds of changes in the distribution of jobs and public and private investment needed to reverse them. These conclusions had been incorporated in the government's White Paper. But none had explored very deeply how such changes could be made. Where did the particular problems of inner city neighbourhoods fit into the wider context of social and economic problems; and how did that affect the political support for meeting the inner city's needs?

In this chapter I turn to the larger problems of social policy which circumscribed the inner city policies of government. The difficulties these policies faced gradually eroded the ideological framework within which the controversies over community action had been fought; and out of this a fundamentally different context of political action is emerging. This chapter is concerned with the disintegration of a conception of social policy which has prevailed in Britain for nearly forty years, the next with alternatives for its reconstruction.

As the Community Development Project evolved, the ideological differences between Home Office officials and many of the Project teams deepened, but they still shared a commitment to the urgency of helping the most disadvantaged. However radically they might disagree about strategies of change, both relied on the argument that social inequity and deprivation ought to be central concerns of policy. Reformers like Derek Morrell and radicals like Jan O'Malley appealed to the same sense of society's moral responsibility to gain political support and public sympathy. They both relied on these social ideals prevailing, and in this they needed each other's help, even though their ideologies drove them apart. This ambivalent mutual dependence profoundly influenced their strategies.

Derek Morrell, introducing community development to the Ditchley Conference, had been preoccupied with the legitimation of policy. How was government, confronted by accumulating evidence of failure, to restore consent for a workable compromise between the demands of social equity and economic growth? Several years earlier, Paul Ylvisaker of the Ford Foundation had presented the Foundation's grey area programmes in the context of a politics where, as he put it, 'won't power' was so outweighing 'will power' as to frustrate any coherent remedy for social deprivation. Both believed, with a deep if troubled

faith in the adaptibility and humanity of liberal democracy, that
their societies were compassionate, responsible and patient
enough to find a way forward. They were looking for ways to
draw poor people out of their estrangement from society, and
administrators out of their self-enclosed, stultifying preoccupation with the maintenance of bureaucratic structures, so as to
regain the momentum of reform. To provoke government responsiveness to this approach, they had to show that much needed
to be done; that poor people wanted it done; and that lack of
imagination, rather than overriding constraints, prevented it
from being done. For this they needed a skilled professional
staff who could mediate between poor people and government,
articulating relevant proposals which the poor would endorse
and government accept. So the Community Development Project
teams were selected from men and women who seemed competent both to direct imaginative experiments and to develop
community organization. They were expected to be advocates
for the poor as well as professionally responsible. The Home
Office was unruffled by radical rhetoric so long as it could be
seen as a way of recruiting community pressure and enthusiasm
for essentially practical actions. In the same way, the Docklands
planners could tolerate and finally support community advocates whose ideology was more radical than their own, for the
sake of a negotiated plan which alienated none of its consti-
tuencies.

This political strategy of reform, therefore, created a context
in which radical advocates could find a legitimate opportunity
and a limited tolerance. They needed time, money and respect-
able sponsors to help foster the kinds of alliances and campaigns
which could lead towards more fundamental changes, just as
reformers needed organizers and advocates who could articulate
the anger and frustration of deprived communities in terms of
policies and plans. Both took for granted a political context in
which government's responsibility to fight poverty and social
inequity was morally unchallengable. So within both government
and the community the controversies over strategy tended to be
preoccupied with the dilemmas created by this ambivalent
interdependence. For reforming civil servants like Morrell, the
problem was to control the impetus for change so that it did not
fall so much into the hands of radical activists as to alienate
local government, or so into the clutches of defensive bureau-
cracy as to alienate community support. For workers in the community, the problem was to avoid being co-opted and constrained
by dependence on public funds and sponsorship, without being
isolated with so few resources that all one's energy went into
scrimping together enough money and members to survive. In
the broadest sense, the problem of action was to translate social
ideals into practicable steps without losing a sense of direction
and progress: and this is what proved ultimately to be so intractable a problem from either point of view.

But in their preoccupation with these issues they were less

aware that the constituency for the social ideals they shared
was disintegrating. Radical critics of liberal policies, and community advocates protesting to more or less liberal governments,
did not need to justify concern for the disadvantaged. They
could use the leverage of government's own explicit commitments
to press for more effective policies. They assumed, I think,
that the commitment of society as a whole to ideals of compassion and progressive equality was independent of liberal policies
- or even more, that these policies were often insincere evasions
of that commitment. Once inauthenticity was exposed, public
opinion would turn towards support for more fundamental and
sustained reforms. But in practice, the ideals were so bound up
in the rationalizations of policy that when the policies failed,
the ideals tended to be discredited, too. This has created a
crisis of legitimation for the liberal tradition within both
Conservative and Labour government, leaving its radical opponents exposed to a conservative reaction against which they
were not prepared. They have now to find a new alliance of
forces and a new framework of ideals, in which to reassert a
consensus of commitment to equality and the needs of the most
disadvantaged. The next chapter discusses these issues of
ideological reconstruction. But first I want to trace how the
intractable problems of unemployment, inflation and rising
public costs led liberal policy through successive rationalizations
which at last undermined its credibility. The rest of this chapter, therefore, explores how government has tried to deal with
two crucial sources of insecurity - the fear of unemployment
and the fear of inflation.

EMPLOYMENT

When the Coventry Community Development Project came to an
end in 1975, John Benington and some of his fellow workers
founded the Coventry Workshop to 'explore the links, in concept and practice, between industry and the community' working primarily 'at the level of shop stewards committees and
grass-roots community groups'.[1] The situation that the Workshop confronted represents some of the characteristic problems
of the British economy as a whole. The largest single employer
in Coventry is the British Leyland Motor Corporation - an
amalgamation of companies forced together by the pressures
of international competition, struggling with the aid of government, which now virtually controls it, against the threat of
bankruptcy. The growing concentration of power in the motor
industry overshadows the city, and suggested to the Coventry
Workshop one way in which, by encouraging analysis and
discussion, it could connect the insecurities of the city's least
protected residents to far more pervasive risks of social and
economic disintegration. The workshop helped to prepare two
documents - *A Workers' Enquiry into the Motor Industry*,[2]

produced by the Institute for Workers' Control, and a paper on
the crisis in Chrysler's British subsidiary, submitted by shop
stewards and staff representatives to the government[3] - which
present the dangers inherent in the manipulation of international
capital as workers' saw them. The same pressures for competitive rationalization underlay the decay of Docklands neighbourhoods - the international reorganization of the sugar and gar-
ment industries; ITT's reallocation of production amongst its
British subsidiaries; the Port of London Authority's concentration of dock work at Tilbury to compete with continental as much
as with other British ports. Each of the cities in which Community Development Projects had been instituted had suffered
the consequences of similar industrial reorganization. The
evolution of the motor industry illustrates forces shaping all
the crucial sectors of the economy.

In 1964, the Ford Motor Company in America introduced the
'Mustang', a stylish car designed to appeal to a newly prosperous younger generation. Over the preceding three and a half
years, it had spent nine million dollars on engineering and
styling and fifty million tooling up for production.[4] Such an
investment presupposed that the costs of production, the
prices of materials and the demand to be stimulated could all be
predicted several years ahead; and implied very extensive
control over the relationships on which profitable production
depended. Ten years after the Mustang's conception, the company undertook another new departure in its line of models -
the 'Fiesta'. But while the Mustang was still an American-built
car for a buoyant American market, the Fiesta was to be a
truly international model, in both design and production.

For this project, Ford is estimated to have spent over a thousand million dollars on research and development alone.[5] The
Fiesta was a carefully calculated rival to German, French and
Italian popular small cars. The company planned to turn out
at least half a million Fiestas a year, as many or more than each
of the principal models with which it was designed to compete,
although the European motor industry already had an average
over-capacity of 30 per cent. Ford expected to thrust its way
into this already crowded market by engineering a lighter,
simpler and thus cheaper car; and by distributing its production internationally, to make the best of labour costs and
concentrate the manufacture of components in separate, highly
automated plants. The car was assembled in England, Germany
and principally at a new factory in Spain; carburettors and
distributors were made in Northern Ireland; gear boxes, trans-
missions and axles at two plants in France.[6]

Such a level of rationalization, investment and international
co-ordination presumes a power to predict crucial relationships,
to manoeuvre within a range of choices, circumventing political
or industrial unrest, so much greater than the Mustang required
as to imply a different order of economic control. Such power
threatens the survival of all but its most powerful rivals. It

could upset national economies and undermine whole cities. As John Benington had pointed out, behind the uncertainties of Coventry's marginal neighbourhoods lay the wider risk that, as the centre of British-owned motor manufacture, the city's economy would undergo continual attrition.

In the face of these dangers, trade unions turned to government, in the hope that its resources and powers of economic regulation could stand up to the forces of international corporate reorganization. But government does not control the relationships on which the survival of a manufacturing centre depends, and so cannot guarantee that the capital it provides to rescue national subsidiaries will be used by its international owners to sustain it. So, for instance, the British government approved the sale of Rootes – a failing British car manufacturer – to the Chrysler Corporation, on the understanding that the American company would revitalize it with fresh capital and management. The President of Chrysler International promised a new model each year. Then, when the company found itself in difficulties, the government provided capital. But Chrysler was soon protesting again that strikes, excessive wages and low productivity were making its British operations unprofitable, and applied for a further injection of government funds. Yet, as it seemed to the workers, these arguments covered a systematic stripping of assets from the British company to the advantage of its operations elsewhere. No new models had been developed; instead, British teams were used to design cars for production in France – and while British dealers were offered incentives to sell French-made models, continental dealers were required to discriminate against British products. The report by shop stewards and staff representatives claimed that 'between 1970 and 1973 the fixed capital employed in Chrysler (UK) was allowed to drift down from $53 million to $46 million. The entire stock of plant and machinery on Chrysler's British factory floors was shown in 1973 to have the incredibly low book value of under $19 million' and continued to decline. Its British plants had 'the lowest fixed capital per man of any Chrysler's subsidiaries[17] – about half that of its French plants. Machinery in some factories was so run-down that breakdown costs were rising rapidly. Meanwhile, tools and machines were being transferred to subsidiaries abroad. At the same time, although the company denied it, the shop stewards' report cited evidence to suggest that Chrysler was deliberately manipulating prices to transfer its profits to countries with lower taxes than Britain. Finally, in 1978, Chrysler announced the sale of its British subsidiary to Peugeot-Citroen, and the government had once again, like the harassed father of an unlucky bride, to question the honourable intentions of a new suitor.

But if government could readily be outmanoeuvred by private corporations, it was not necessarily any better placed by nationalization, despite the urging of organized workers. Public or private, a corporation inhibited from exploiting internationally

the cheapest labour, the greatest economies of scale and auto-
mation, the most rational distribution of its assets and profits,
was likely to go under. Either a state-owned company was free,
like British Petroleum, to pursue its business much as any
other competitor,[8] or it became, like British Leyland, a liability
which would ultimately have to be accounted for as a drain on
public resources. Nationalization was not, in itself, a means of
protecting employment, but of rescuing a national industry.
Government support of British Leyland was conditional upon
union agreement to reduce labour and boost productivity, and
its plans looked forward to a halving of the workforce.

So the experience of the British motor industry faced its
workers with a dilemma. Socially responsive public ownership
was the traditional answer to the threatening manipulations of
international corporate power. Support within the trade union
movement and the Labour Party could be mobilized behind it.
No other response seemed capable of subordinating economic
decisions to social purposes. Yet in practice, nationalization
only seemed to co-opt workers into accepting, under public
management, the same attrition of their numbers and bargaining
power which they had rejected from corporate hands. It could
not change the overriding logic of economic rationalization, only
the agents who took the blame for its social consequences. Hence
the connections between industrial reorganization and social
hardships, which the Coventry Workshop was trying to articulate, did not lead to a coherent political strategy. As the Joint
Docklands Action Group had concluded, if the solutions depended on public enterprise, any foreseeable government intervention was bound to betray the hope that it would arrest the
attrition of manufacturing employment. At the same time, the
traditional socialist preoccupation with public control of production and finance distracted attention from other, far more
influential policies by which government *had* sought to protect
security of employment. These policies were changing the structure of employment, the alignment of class interests, and the
critical tensions within society almost as profoundly as the
international reorganization of production.

Throughout the decade when the most spectacular agglomera-
tions of capital were taking place, government expenditure on
non-marketable goods and services was growing equally remark-
ably, and so was public employment. 'A revolution, a great
structural shift in employment, has occurred in the British
economy since about 1962...in just ten years employment outside industry increased by almost one-third relative to employment in industry, and...this increase was predominantly in the
public sector.'[9] Between 1961 and 1973 jobs in local government
grew by 54 per cent; in central government by 14 per cent;
outside government by only 7 per cent. The greatest increase –
74 per cent – was in education. Similar changes were taking
place in the United States. Between 1950 and 1970, when the
workforce as a whole grew by 37 per cent, university and

college teachers multiplied 291 per cent, other teachers, 146
per cent.[10] In roughly the same period, expenditures by all
levels of government had nearly doubled as a proportion of
the national product.[11] In both countries - taking defence industries into account - about a third of all workers were now
directly or indirectly on the public payroll.

These increases, in both Britain and the United States, were
justified largely as the foundation on which to sustain economic
growth. Since the early 1960s, human capital theory had been
drawing attention to the importance of investments in education
as a component of productivity.[12] Education - and especially
higher education - was to expand to ensure the skills and new
knowledge for continuing technological innovation. The British
Committee on Higher Education, chaired by Lord Robbins,
argued for new universities by comparing the British production
of highly trained skills with her industrial rivals. Harold Wilson,
campaigning for the Labour Party in 1964, promised the 'white
heat' of technological progress. In the United States, towards
the end of the decade, as funds poured into universities,
academics inspired by the heady rhetoric of the 'post-industrial
society' began to identify the 'knowledge industry' as the
crucial asset of the economy - and rebellious students, suspicious of its purposes, were equally convinced of the university's
central importance.

Defence expenditure could be justified as fulfilling a complementary purpose: it upheld the balance of power which sheltered
nations open to the expansion of capitalist economies from
absorption into a less receptive, slower growing, Russian-
dominated sphere of influence. Other costs, in welfare and the
provision of social services might be less obviously productive,
but they secured democratic consent for the progress of economic rationalization - both by distributing the rewards of growth
in services that everyone wanted and by taking care of the
casualties of economic change.

Looked at sympathetically, the changing structure of employment could be seen as a national response to the demands of
a prosperous society. As people had more money, they spent
more of it on services and less on increasing their material
possessions. They wanted education; better health, sharper
vision and more regular teeth; they became more compassionate,
setting higher standards for the well-being of the poor and
handicapped; and these demands could often best be met by
public provisions. Looked at less benignly, the changes responded to the need of capital for skills, research, infrastructure, social and spatial reorganization to facilitate its further
accumulation.[13] Either way, the new employments came to be
regarded as useful, even necessary, to the progress of capitalist
society.

But when their eventual contribution is looked at more closely,
these public expenditures seem essentially, if partly unconsciously, to represent as much a compensation for the declining

labour requirements of the most productive private sectors, as a response either to their needs, or to the wishes of the public at large. Did the expansion of education, for instance, really sustain the productivity of the economy, or provide something intrinsically desired? When the British government raised the compulsory school-leaving age by a year, to sixteen, despite overcrowded classes and a shortage of teachers, what gain in productivity could it foresee? Where were all the graduates of the innovative courses, launched by new and expanding universities in their confident years, to make a contribution which they could not have made without them? Broadening the scope of the educational pyramid, drawing more and more students into higher levels, has continually lengthened its apex, so that higher qualifications and more degrees are required for jobs that once accepted less. The expansion of education was not, therefore, in any simple, unambiguous way a response to a growing demand for education itself. Young people, even though they enjoy learning, necessarily look at education instrumentally, as a means to a career. They become bored and impatient with it when it leads nowhere, because it then seems like play, holding them back from growing up. Another year at school in itself could mean only a year of restless boredom. The demand for more education is mostly a demand for access to career opportunities for which educational qualifications have become a more and more exclusive prerequisite. Often these elaborated theoretical preparations are not really investments in training more productive skills, but thresholds which regulate access to a vocation or profession. Nor does more sophisticated management of production typically require more educated people. Often rationalized, more capital-intensive production simplifies tasks so that plants are closed, skilled workers dismissed, and production relocated in areas where a smaller, less skilled labour force can be employed at lower wages.

Not that educational policy was consciously designed to absorb unemployment. Rather, as young people found they were unemployable without higher educational qualifications, the pressure to provide more opportunities for education grew. Certificates of schooling are crude but universal measures of competence, social conformity, and class: they provide employers with ready-made thresholds by which to define the pool of recruitable applicants for jobs. What the applicants have learned may be much less important than the evidence that they had the competitive staying power, the social advantages and the talent to learn it. But this relationship, whereby the length of education increases in response to the scarcity of employment, comes to be seen in reverse, as a need for more and more education in order to qualify for employment, and so to the fallacy that the unemployed could find work if only they had more schooling. Hence government policies to relieve poverty, especially amongst young people, in both Britain and the United States, concentrated on education and vocational training.

Though this may achieve a marginally fairer distribution of
opportunity between classes or races, it contributes most to
the relief of unemployment by withdrawing more young people
for longer from the search for jobs, and stimulating careers
in education.

Similarly, the expansion of public employment was not crudely
making work, but the outcome of complex and conflicting pressures. Even when a policy was undertaken explicitly to create
jobs - as, for instance, when the British government made
grants for public construction works, or the American government legislated a federally funded programme to retrain redundant aeronautical engineers as administrators of social services[14]
- it would scarcely have been legitimate unless it seemed useful. For the most part, the growth of occupations was justified
by the social ideals to which they contributed - training talent,
improving health, strengthening the nation, research of all
kinds, reintegrating alienated members of society into the ethos
of work and self-sufficiency. And these justifications might be
grounded in evident needs: more children require more schools,
more old people call for more services for the elderly, changing
technologies of warfare demand yet more sophisticated means of
evasion and counter-terror. But once occupations were created,
they developed a constituency, organization and rationale for
their own survival. Since they were not promoted, in the first
instance, merely as make-work projects, they could not be
carelessly abandoned when to make such work seemed either
unnecessary or too costly. Each had a purpose, endorsed by
legislation, that it was mandated to fulfil; and the pursuit of
that purpose naturally generated more claims on resources as
time went by. Why shut up shop when you have just landed
triumphantly on the moon and the planets beckon? Why abandon
the relief of poverty, just as you have discovered its extent
and problems? As the Seebohm Committee realized, rationalizing
and co-ordinating British social welfare services, just because
it made them more efficient, would at first expose more clearly
the unmet needs. Research notoriously generates more research;
education reveals how widespread ignorance and illiteracy are;
medical services discover new possibilities of treatment; planning articulates more complex and exacting demands for the
reconciliation of social, economic and environmental goals. Each
vocation acquired the momentum of its own evolving purposes.

The distribution of occupations therefore reflected the
accumulating expectations of a society in which government had
become a more and more crucial mediator of employment chances.
But these expectations were both competitive and partly contradictory. Schematically, the dilemma can be set out as follows:
the prevailing ideology recognizes a national level of unemployment which, though it varies from nation to nation and from time
to time, is acceptable as normal. When the actual rate rises
much above this, many people feel threatened. Even if their
jobs are not immediately at risk, a rising rate projects a more

precarious future. No government can ignore abnormalities
which alarm a large part of the electorate without undermining
its claim to deserve power. Yet it cannot resolve one abnorma-
lity by creating another. It must balance the expectation that
it will restore a normal rate of employment against the expectation that it will sustain the normal working of the economy.
Ideally, then, it would generate employment by stimulating
economic growth: both British and American governments reiterated this constantly as their fundamental policy. But in
practice, experience shows that sustained growth depends on
international competitiveness, and competitiveness requires the
shaking out of redundant workers and the closing of inefficient
plant. Direct intervention, as with the British government's
nationalization of endangered industries, leads to politically
embarrassing plans to reduce employment. Indirect intervention
to stimulate domestic demand risks inflation and a worsening
balance of trade, upsetting the future prospects of international
competitiveness. At the same time, structural reforms in the
economy, even if they would ultimately benefit the employment
rate, are too slow in taking effect to satisfy the immediate
demand for jobs. Government therefore has to find more employment in sectors where the need to calculate competitive profitability is not so direct. Yet it still has to justify these expenditures in terms of the eventual well-being of society, whose
wealth and possibilities of social justice are seen to depend on
its competitiveness within an international market. It therefore
promotes publicly financed employment in activities which have
already become institutionalized as social investments in economic potency.

The association between higher education and industrial competitiveness, for instance, was conceived long before the
Robbins Committee. Nineteenth-century British reformers had
argued for the revival of moribund scientific research and
teaching at Oxford and Cambridge, inferring a threat to British
pre-eminence inherent in the more modern French and German
polytechnics; the new industrial cities established colleges and
universities to train technicians. Urban redevelopment and slum
clearance, too, has always been as much a means of realizing
potential land values as an endeavour of public health, welfare
or civic pride. The British reorganization of local government,
both technically and structurally, in the 1960s was inspired
partly by the desire to introduce into public management the
organizing skills and philosophy of corporate business. None
of these reforms, nor their American counterparts, were conceived of, in themselves, as means of providing compensatory
employment for society at large; rather as necessary investments in the social foundations of the nation's future prosperity.
In retrospect, it becomes apparent that this changing occupa-
tional structure has enabled manufacturing to rationalize its
use of labour without an alarming increase in unemployment.
And this has three crucial consequences: first, to maintain a

high rate of employment in society as a whole, the public sector must sustain the workforce it has absorbed, since it now accounts for so substantial a proportion; second, an ideology has evolved which legitimates public expenditures as productive investments in social infrastructure for a technically sophis- ticated, 'post-industrial' society; and third, once the unemploy- ment rate rises, compensatory increases in public employment have a ready-made rationale.

But even if these social investments are indeed productive, they clearly cannot be undertaken with a precision, timing or control comparable to investments in the private sector. Young people cannot be fed into education with any guarantee that they will emerge with the particular skills in demand; but they themselves will still demand an occupation for their talents. No reorganization of social services can predict when, or at how great a cost, it may succeed in incorporating more disadvantaged people into the mainstream of the economy. The rehabilitation of Docklands or New York, as a centre of international finance and government, projects ambitious public works for roads, slum clearance, retraining, with only a guess at the returns it might generate in an indeterminate future. The relationships are far looser, more speculative, and more aggregated as pos- sibilities than any investment for profit.

At the same time, this broadly conceived integration of social purposes with economic competitiveness tends to overwhelm the earlier distinction between economic management and social redistribution, where each is seen as a separate, complementary field of action. Social provisions are no longer justified as goods in their own right - better houses, health, more compassionate care - but as nationally productive investments in adaptability and morale. While he was director of the Coventry Community Development Project, John Benington wrote a paper entitled 'Government Becomes Big Business' - pointing to the city government's preoccupation with industrial promotion, but presidents and prime ministers too are dwindling into the senior accountants of the national business. The growth of public employment is therefore doubly vulnerable to ideological disaf- fection, because its economic value often cannot easily be substantiated either as an investment or as a response to what people most want. It represents, rather, a plausible rationaliza- tion of the only means of maintaining employment as a whole within the government's grasp. And this solution cannot be sustained, once the second insecurity - inflation - becomes uppermost in people's mind.

INFLATION

If public expenditure compensates for the dwindling proportion of the workforce the market economy absorbs, holding for a while a balance between the reorganization of capital and acceptable rates of unemployment, then it cannot – even if it were technically possible – undergo a corresponding rationalization of the use of labour, without undermining its contribution to public confidence in job security. Yet public employees have a right to expect wages in line with comparable occupations in the private sector, since their work is represented as equally valuable. Since there are no comparable increases in the productivity of their labour, the relative costs of public employment tend to rise, even without further expansion.[15] That is, the surplus created by more capital-intensive production tends to be redistributed, as a whole, not in wages to the workers at these machines – since there are proportionately fewer of them – but in higher wages to public employees doing no more than before, through the medium of higher tax revenues. If government tries to resist this pressure by discriminating against wages in the public sector, it creates an intolerable inequity.

The distribution of wages is conventional – a set of traditional expectations as to the relative rewards of different kinds of work, shaped by the historical circumstances in which an occupation arose and established its frame of reference. As John Dunlop has described it,[16] this distribution can be seen in terms of clusters, which relate the pay of various jobs within an organization to a key function, and contours, which relate the wage scales of comparable activities to each other. So, for instance, the wages for working at the coal-face sets the standard by which other mine work is graduated: surface jobs pay less, supervisory jobs more. At the same time, miners compare their wages to skilled men in engineering or ship-building. These clusters and contours are liable to drift, and they may not have any obvious justification, beyond their familiarity and acceptance. But in practice, they are constantly referred to in wage negotiations as yardsticks against which to measure the inequity of unfavourable changes. No group of workers is likely to accept a fall in their wage as fair unless it is shared equally by everyone.

On the other hand, a group of workers in a strong position to bargain for a relative increase in their wages – because their skills are scarce, or in return for agreeing to more intensive methods of production – is unlikely to hold back. Nor do their employers have much incentive to resist, since they need to attract them, to buy off disruptive resistance to reorganization, and they expect the higher wages (which may be passed on in higher prices) to pay off in profitability. Hence wages rise in the strongest sectors of the economy, distorting the familiar contours of distribution, and provoking demands from everybody else for equitable upward adjustment. Government cannot therefore regulate wages in the public sector, where the potential tax burden is critical, without a generalized wages policy, directed above all towards the leading private employers and the unions of their workers. The campaign against inflationary

wage increases is drawn into protesting increases which both
labour and management are ready to agree, and which may not,
in themselves, be inflationary at all. No such campaign can
survive for long against the united interests of the most powerful employers and organized workers. And the risks of insisting,
even where the employer is a public authority, are dramatically
illustrated by the miners' strike which toppled Edward Heath's
Conservative government.

The National Coal Board and the miners' union were ready to
negotiate wage increases substantially above the statutory
limits set by government policy. They disagreed marginally
as to the relative increases within the cluster; the Board wanted
above all to attract coal-face workers, the union demanded
comparable raises for the surface workers, who were the majority of its members. Both agreed that rising oil prices made
coal competitive again, and the industry needed and could
afford to attract new recruits to a skilled, hard, and dangerous
job. But the union's crucial claim was equity: miners, once
ranked amongst the best-paid skilled manual workers, had
sunk to eighteenth place. The government could not afford to
acknowledge any of this case: if it allowed a nationalized industry to flout its guidelines, the whole campaign for wage limita-
tion would lose all credibility. It tried every device to mobilize
public opinion behind its stand - lectured, threatened, engin-
eered a fuel crisis, closing factories for two days a week,
cutting power supplies, even shortening the hours of television.
Finally it called a general election on the issue. But it lost.
People sympathized with the miners' claim. They did not
regard such obstinate interference in wage negotiations as
either fair or legitimate.

Any government, faced with the need to hold back the wages
of public employment, is caught in a tangle of ideological con-
fusions.[17] For the sake of economic competitiveness, it ought
to encourage high wages where they would facilitate more intensive and profitable production. But it cannot do so without
increasing the cost of public services, unless it argues that
policemen or firemen or nurses have less right to improve their
standard of living, or defend it against inflation, than someone
who screws bolts into a chassis on an assembly line. Wage policies have, then, to represent some universal principles of
equity. But the prevailing pattern of wages does not conform
to any principle that can readily be articulated and reinforced:
it is not a simple outcome of supply and demand, nor graduated
according to the social value of the work, nor a return for
what people have invested in training their own talents, nor
a compensation for hardship and danger, nor equal. Any of
these principles may reinforce a claim, but in incoherent,
inconsistent ways: university professors, educated at public
expense, are still paid more than miners, though they face no
greater danger than a sour review of their latest book. The
market in skills and labour is constricted by powerful organiza-

tions which inhibit competition by claims of status, by gender and racial discrimination, by the vocational identities to which we become attached. Hence the only principle of equity available to government which would not involve – in one way or another – a radical revision of the whole existing pattern of distribution is the principle that controls should affect everyone's familiar expectation of the relative standing of their job about equally. But since some have been falling behind their expectations, while others have just won a raise or are about to achieve it, even this principle is difficult to carry out fairly. The wage policies of governments therefore end up appealing to an over-riding national interest in accordance with principles which are often incoherent, fundamentally arbitrary, and bear down unfairly on those with least power to resist. But weak and short-lived as they are, they threaten above all the economic security of public employees against whom they are most insistently directed, and provoke them into stronger organization.

All government-financed occupations have come to recognize that their future depends on capturing their full share of a growing public revenue, and mobilize to protect their status, recognition, and vocational ideals. They cannot any longer trust to the traditional security of the public servant and they begin to adopt the tough bargaining tactics of the best organized trade unions. Teachers, firemen, police, garbage collectors, nurses and doctors come out on strike. Even such dignified mandarins as British civil servants or university professors threaten to join the picket lines. Those who discover how uncomfortably disruptive for society their strikes can be, learn to lever their wages to unexpectedly high levels, irrespective of the eventual ability of their employer to pay, aggravating the sense of grievance of less immediately and obviously necessary workers. Hence the relative cost of public employment rises, not only from the movement of wages which set the reference points of everyone's expectations, but in reaction against the threat to these expectations implied by policies of wage control. When these policies fail to limit wages as a whole, or to resist the organized pressure of public employees against unfair discrimination, government is faced with an uncomfortable choice. It must either increase its tax revenue, run into inflationary debt, or abruptly dismantle the whole complex structure by which pressures to rationalize the competitive economy have been reconciled with security of employment. It is the collapse of the first two solutions which eventually drives Britain to drastic retrenchment or New York City into virtual receivership under the exemplary discipline of bankers.[18]

TAXES

Sooner or later, if wage controls cannot restrain it, the cost of maintaining employment comes up against the practicable

limits of taxation. Inflation and recession compound the inherent difficulty of persuading people, either as producers or
users, to go on paying increasing taxes to support public
employment, irrespective of its intrinsic value. From the point
of view of international corporations, taxes correspond to rent
for location: if the price is too high for the amenities provided,
they can arrange to rent less space in that city, region, or
nation, bargain for more favourable terms, or avoid payment.
The burden of high taxation can be passed on or partly evaded
by higher prices, cross-jurisdictional transfers of capital and
profits, by manipulating subsidies and migrating from high-tax
areas. The less the fortunes of business are bound up with
the prosperity or political stability of any particular place, the
less the incentive to pay for social investments designed to
promote the economic competitiveness of that city or nation -
especially if the economic relevance of these investments is
undemonstrable. Other locations already promise the cheaper
labour, the convenient sites and necessary social infrastructure
at less cost. The more detached from spatial commitment business becomes, the more it can play off taxes as it plays off
labour or supplies, without regard for the consequences, beyond
the period in which it has calculated the profit on an investment
anywhere will mature. Any business whose affairs are bent to
a patriotic purpose is at a disadvantage. In the end it has to
choose between political cynicism or failure. Hence nationalization, instead of offering an alternative model of socially responsible management, becomes unfairly tarnished with a reputation
for incompetence.

There remains, of course, a large part of business activity
and capital which cannot choose its place. But just because it
cannot so readily evade the burden of taxation, it becomes less
profitable, attracts less investment and weakens. In its own
defence, it must try to attract back the international pace-
setters of economic growth, who alone have the power to revali-
date the capital locked in land and property. Hence the quality
of life is a less urgent concern than to restore, as ruthlessly
as need be, the competitive conditions for reinvestment - tax
incentives, a disciplined and undemanding workforce, the
retrenchment of social welfare, and amenities for the corporate
elite. The civic pride and social responsibility of an enlightened
chamber of commerce gives way to the pressure of an international market.

Yet this manipulation generates popular resentment, not
against business, but above all against government. In the first
place, government characteristically reacts to the rising costs
of public services by a peculiarly frustrating compromise: it
at once raises tax revenues and trims provisions, so that
communities pay more for less. And because so large a part of
costs are independent of rate of use, the cuts tend to represent poor value for money, increasing the burden of overheads
on remaining services. To save a custodian's wages, a building

is closed to community use, and a whole range of activities are
frustrated. So with public transportation, libraries, services of
all kinds - they are less available but cost more. Although
there are fewer schoolchildren, and reports document a progressive decline in educational performance, schools constantly
need more money. It seems perverse, yet the angrier people
become, and the more pressure they bring to bear for immediately visible savings, the greater the chances that resources
will be wasted or under-used. In practice, greater efficiency
is likely to mean more rather than less investment, as the public service professions argue. School teachers want higher
salaries to sustain the morale and quality of their vocation, and
smaller classes so that they can at last provide a decent education. But the force of this argument is undermined by a pervasive mistrust of the rationalizations by which government
has sought to justify growing public employment.

To legitimate public expenditure as a social investment in
productivity sets altogether unrealistic standards of performance. Investment implies a greater return - a ratio of costs to
benefits which can in some way be calculated as profitable.
The more government expenditures are conceived of not as
goods in their own right, but as contributions to the creation
of future goods, the more public management adopts accounting
methods analogous to private corporations, inviting corresponding measures of efficiency. So, for instance, the American
anti-poverty programmes were subject to a series of evaluations
which attempted to measure the return on investment, in terms
of their stated goals. How many newly productive workers
were created, at what costs, by all the vocational training,
remedial education, community enterprises, innovative treatment of juvenile delinquents, and social rehabilitation? By
these standards, the measurable achievements were at best
ambiguous and generally discouraging. The programmes helped
some poor people; they provided jobs, access to political careers
and legal aid to communities who had been excluded; stimulated
a campaign for welfare rights; sometimes gave rise to organizations able to veto or amend disruptive local plans. But these
small gains of a difficult justice are irrelevant to the claims of
policy. The public hears only that the programmes were failures
in their own terms, certified by rigorous social accounting.

Correspondingly, if universities are investments in knowledge
- human capital for a technologically sophisticated society -
where is the purposeful army of efficient problem-solvers they
were promised to produce? Any comprehensive, lively, liberal
centre of learning will turn out a disorderly rabble of social
critics, scholars, self-serving careerists, rebels, drop outs,
artists, as well as competent technicians - all demanding employment for their talents; which may be all to the good, but it is
not, I think, what taxpapers were encouraged to support. The
same questions can be asked of research. Populist politicians
have only to read, selectively, from the topics supported out of

public funds, to ridicule the pretensions that they serve any useful purpose - and government itself begins to look more closely at the productive relevance ot the inquiries that it finances. In practice, this strict accounting destroys the imaginative idiosyncrasy from which the most fruitful ideas come. But policy is trapped by the terms in which it has sought its legitimation.

So people come to see that government spending is both incompetent and exploitative - a boondoggle for professional poverty experts, neighbourhood hustlers, self-serving academicians, bureaucrats whose careers are vested in its perpetuation; the province of an educated middle-class whose liberal prejudices it hypocritically serves, and who escape with good salaries into comfortable suburbs where they do not even share fairly the burden of their cost. It does not matter that their counterparts in private corporations are certainly richer and probably no less likely to be self-serving, extravagant or incompetent. Private enterprise appears efficient by the crucial test on which public employment fails. It makes a profit on its investments. The comparison, misleading in itself, is reinforced by corporate propaganda. But the widespread belief, in both Britain and the United States, that public work is inefficient, padded with unnecessary exployees, over-paid and self-inflating arises from the perception that it is not simply a response to popular demand, nor a necessary contribution to national defence or the competitiveness of city or nation. The growth of public spending represents a much more complex compromise between pressures to compensate for the disruptive consequences of the reorganization of capital; pressure from public employees themselves for status and security; pressures for more planning, administration and public relations to handle the increasingly pervasive interventions of government; as well as demands for services, amenities and social infrastructure. The pattern of employment which results has, besides, the political and bureaucratic inertia of all structures in which people's lives are invested. It becomes very hard to justify as a whole, and so can provoke a powerful alliance of business interests and public opinion against government spending, to which government itself can find no adequate defence within the framework of its own ideology.

LEGITIMATION

I have tried to suggest how the reorganization of labour within the leading sectors of the economy, the corresponding growth of public employment, inflation and a growing resentment against taxation combine to undermine a conception of policy of which the American anti-poverty programmes, the Community Development Project and the redevelopment of Docklands are all small parts. This conception presented public expenditure

essentially as a social investment in structural change rather
than the redistribution of growth in cash and kind. It attempted
to reconcile policies which promoted the concentration and
rationalization of capital into internationally competitive organizations, with a counterbalancing public investment to rein-
corporate the regions, communities and kinds of people whom
growth had abandoned. But the balance could only be sustained
so long as public expenditure at an increasing rate was compatible with the continued attraction of investment, on the one
hand, and an ideological tolerance of taxation, on the other.
These costs could not be contained effectively by wage control,
since discrimination against the public sector and interference
in bargaining in the market sector both proved politically intolerable for long. Nor could the rate of economic restructuring
be held back without threatening the growth on which public
expenditure rested. Even without other inflationary factors,
therefore, the constant pressure on the public sector to absorb
the social costs of continual capital reorganization on so vast
a scale seems ultimately overwhelming.

The se problems are compounded by the growing numbers of
people looking for work, especially women. Changes in house-
hold composition – higher rates of divorce, more people living
independently – create more people who depend on their own
earnings, and most married women now work too, to keep up
the standard of the family's living. As more women seek paid
work and households become organized around the ability to
maintain these earnings, the structure of the labour market
adapts to take advantage of their vulnerability and lower
expectations. This tends to displace better paid workers from
production, increasing the pressure on the public sector to
create compensatory opportunities.

Worldwide inflation and recession only aggravate the inherent
instability of a resolution whose costs, and the inability to
meet them, are bound to increase. The fiscal crisis cannot be
postponed indefinitely, and the vulnerability of the claims
for social expenditure are exposed. For whatever the virtues
of the education, the services, plans, research, community
developments, financed from public funds, no investment which
drives its maker towards bankruptcy is a success. Economic
viability no longer seems to depend on incorporating the
wasted talents and resources of society, but on the competitive
attraction of capital at whatever social cost. Yet, at the same
time, the constituency whose jobs depend on public expenditure
is still large, well-organized and politically insistent; and its
work can often claim to be more obviously useful or more relevant to the humane ideals of society than profit-making occupations. The conflict of expectations is irreconcilable.

As the ideology which justified the growth of public employment as a productive asset disintegrates, government is left at
the mercy of contradictory pressures from its electorate which
it has no argument to reconcile. It then faces, in Jurgen

Habermas's phrase, a crisis of legitimation:[19]

> The government budget is burdened with the common costs
> of a more-and-more socialized production....The state
> apparatus is, therefore, faced simultaneously with two
> tasks. On the one hand, it is supposed to raise the requi-
> site amount of taxes by skimming off profits and income
> and to use the available taxes so rationally that crisis
> ridden disturbances of growth can be avoided. On the other
> hand, the selective raising of taxes, the discernible pattern
> of priority in their use, and the administrative performances
> themselves must be so constituted that the need for legiti-
> mation can be satisfied as it arises. If the state fails in the
> former task, there is a deficit in administrative rationality.
> If it fails in the latter task, a deficit in legitimation results.

These crises are no longer hypothetical, but evident in the
growing disillusionment, fickleness and apathy of electoral
democracy.

The failure of governments to sustain a legitimate, coherently
rational defence against the threats of unemployment and inflation reflects their increasing helplessness before the requirements of internationally organized capital. Their theoretically
greater resources and powers of control are inhibited by political and ideological commitments, by jurisdictional boundaries,
by the complex, opportunistic alliances on which their majorities
rest. The resources of corporate capital are by contrast less
committed, unbounded by political jurisdictions, autonomously
directed and free of any responsibility except to return a more-
or-less legal profit to their shareholders. They can therefore
mobilize a power over the prosperity of a community, a region,
even a nation which increasingly intimidates any government
dependent on holding and attracting them. At the same time,
the expectations they have to meet are much simpler - to
produce an abundance of goods at a profit within the law. They
deploy enormous resources to influence these expectations,
and their only institutionalized critics are concerned primarily
with their legal observance or the quality of their goods. Hence
they arouse general anger only when, as in the oil shortage,
the supply falters. Though the social consequences of particular
actions may draw protest from the workers or communities
affected, the general consequences are not attributable to any
enterprise. Capitalists do not have to legitimate their actions
by the collective outcome of capitalism. The only identifiable
authority, responsible for the workings of the economy as a
whole, is still government. So it is against government that
resentment turns - not just because people are fed up with
taxes and a declining quality of service - but in reaction against
its impotence to solve the problems of inflation, unemployment
and sustained growth.

As a convincingly rational, commanding and legitimately

inclusive conception of policy seems less and less within the grasp of any government the political system can produce, the sense that society can collectively articulate its ideals and steer actions coherently towards them becomes attenuated. The whole structure of societal control through which people seek protection and meaning for their lives by the claims of common citizenship begins to seem ineffectual. Membership in society becomes less and less meaningful as a ground of action, for if people no longer believe that government knows how to hold inflation, ensure employment and restore the conditions of a general prosperity, they have no good reason to sacrifice their immediate self-interest to common purposes whose realization cannot be convincingly promised. So they compound the ideological disintegration, as they try to exploit the enormous resources and regulative powers which government represents.

In these circumstances people become divided against each other, and even against themselves. They can only struggle to claim the highest wages, the least taxes, the largest share of public funds, the firmest institutional protection of their jobs they can impose. The connecting ideology that would link these claims to their consequences for others, and ultimately for oneself, is discredited. If corporations manipulate every situation to their competitive advantage, how can the rest of us protect ourselves unless we do likewise? Every argument for restraint seems either a confidence trick, contrived to undermine the force of a claim, or the reiteration of self-stultifying policies which may temporarily relieve one problem only at the expense of another. This disenchantment with the possibilities of government is reflected in fewer votes, incoherent choices, weaker, more opportunistic leadership; the substitution of contrived images for substantial rationality; and the explicit arbitration of public policy by a caucus of the most powerful organized interests.

The disintegration of political rationality, as the expression of shared ideals, hurts most obviously the liberal reformers whose arguments have always depended on it. But it also creates a situation which cannot readily be assimilated to the traditions of radical political struggle. The present crisis is not of capital, nor even essentially of government as a facilitator of capital accumulation, but in all those aspects of government which attempt to compensate for its disruptive consequences through social security, the redirection of economic chances, wage and price control, the maintenance of employment and redistributive taxation. It does not unite most people against the conditions of successful competition in an international capitalistic market, because they are not ready, in their own interest, to abandon a system which has brought them so disproportionate a share of the world's wealth. They are disillusioned with government as much for its failures to sustain the competitiveness of their home territory as for the inadequacy of its social protection. Government appears, so to speak, on both sides of the political equation; on the one hand, it appears as an employer and distributor of resources, against whom workers and claimants must organize and struggle to secure a fairer share of the total surplus of wealth society produces; on the other, it appears as the regulator of the conditions under which that surplus can continue to be produced. When, therefore, radical organization tries to build alliances which draw unions and community groups, public and private employees, workers, the unemployed, the old and handicapped into mutual support, it can demonstrate, analytically, the structural connection between their frustrations. But it cannot derive from that a common strategy in the tradition of industrial or militant community action. Well-organized workers in the leading sectors of the economy can only bargain for progressive wages so long as they accept the attrition of their numbers and the consequences for prices; the trade union movement as a whole can institutionalize greater job security only so long as it accepts diminished chances for those seeking work. Every group, whether it represents public or private employees, taxpayers, community groups, old people can only succeed if it either beggars another, or threatens the economic resourcefulness from which all claims have in the end to be met. Hence mutual sympathy does not translate into mutually supportive action.

Whether political action is articulated as the expression of consensual ideals, or as a struggle to change the balance of advantage between broad classes of society, the inability of government to dominate the conditions under which capital accumulation can continue undermines their coherence as much as government itself. Even more extensive nationalization, as the radical wing of the Labour Party has proposed it, cannot change the international context in which nationalized production has to compete. It suggests no obvious alternative to the logic of rationalization and concentration into supranational, autonomous corporations; and to make their profits public property does not in itself fundamentally alter the constraints on redistributing profits for social purposes, so long as the business still has to rival its competitors' control over labour, materials, financial resources and tax liability.

Once government loses the power to dominate economic relationships, a strategy of class struggle, carried on through the diffuse pressure of industrial and community action, cannot any longer be conceived of as a progressive enlargement of social control, through which the interests of working people can be asserted over capital. It becomes a deliberate attempt to aggravate the crisis of legitimation. By overburdening government with claims which it cannot meet, its inability to wring concessions from capitalist control is made explicit. Unable any longer to satisfy or moderate the expectations of the electorate, it loses the authority of consent, and stands exposed as the repressive agent of corporate economic power.

But what might follow from this is frighteningly unpredictable.
Confronted with an apocalyptic scenario of growing repression
and violent struggle, most people would surely rather knuckle
under to the bleak, uninspiring but familiar compromises of
hard capitalist times.

For all these reasons, the radical critique of community
development and Docklands planning could not evolve a strategy
of action corresponding to its evolving analysis. Its practical
influence, as an argument for the poor and disadvantaged,
depended on the government's need to demonstrate its legitimacy, as a rationally moral and effective arbiter between economic viability and social justice. So long as the ideological framework of policy was attacked only from the left, advocacy and
protest had some purchase. But once radical and reactionary
movements combined to pull apart its tenuous rationality and
threadbare idealism, the growing crisis of legitimation creates
a self-reinforcing disillusionment in which the weakness of
the radical constituency is painfully exposed. The more government is discredited, the less authority it has to moderate claims
upon it in the interests of society as a whole, since no one
any longer has confidence that moderation will be rewarded by
greater security for their expectations. Every interest, in
self-defence, competes to ensure the predictability of the
relationships on which it directly relies. The allocation of
resources then reflects, more and more cynically, the balance
of power. But this generates an even greater insecurity, as
it compounds the weakness of the ideological framework to
which any moral claim upon society must be referred. The need
for some ideological reassertion becomes overwhelming. But
without an extraordinary energy and imagination, diffused
throughout society, the ideological reconstruction will fall into
the hands of those with most power to control relationships –
the practical men of business who, as Marx suggests, most
of the time leave ideology to others. And they will simply
justify the actual structure of power as they are able to assert
it. There is no historical evidence to suggest that such a
reconstruction would be too unpopular or repressive to command
consent.

Yet the appeal of radical ideas is above all, I believe, their
hope of a society less empty of compassion and co-operative
endeavour. The reintegration of meaning and action is finally
a question of the meaning of society itself. What, if anything,
do we all want to belong to? The political and economic pressures, whose interaction I have tried to trace, are not consolidating an overriding class interest. They tend rather to provoke
a disintegrative competition for personal security, from which
the most powerful have most to gain. But if, in Britain and
the United States, most people are not ready to see their
society as a battleground from which a new class domination
will emerge, they are not willing either to see it as only the
instrumental setting in which people compete, according to their

power, for private satisfactions. For then all work, all relationships, even the most altruistic, are corrupted by the
structure which co-opts them. Doing good becomes merely the
gentler side of self-serving control, as doing harm is merely
the rougher side of looking after oneself. The underlying
loneliness of such a world is frightening.

The disintegration of liberal policy therefore also involved
the disintegration of a relationship between government and
social ideals which left the collective meaning of social policy
in desperate need of restatement. In the next chapter, I turn
to the principles which underlay the liberal conception, and the
alternatives that may replace them.

5 PARADIGMS

In his interpretation of the history of science, Thomas Kuhn
introduces the concept of a 'paradigm', as the crucial organizing framework which contains, structures and defines the work
of a scientific profession. When a paradigm breaks down, the
profession undergoes a fundamental transformation in its working assumptions.[1] In much the same sense, the evolution of the
Community Development Project and the Docklands plan can be
seen as reflecting the disintegration of a dominant paradigm
of social policy, which had defined the relationship between
meaning and action for a generation of politicians, administrators, social scientists and reformers.

A paradigm is a set of assumptions about the scope, method
and purpose of a particular science, which determines its
questions, the nature of its evidence and its principles of interpretation. The paradigm gives the work of every scientist its
meaning, by relating it to the work of every other in a collective
enterprise of search, debate and mutual criticism, through
which the science itself makes incontrovertible progress. Though
the particular theories to which the paradigm gives rise, and
which present the recognized problems of research and exploration, are constantly in question, the paradigm itself cannot be
questioned without threatening the enterprise as a whole.
Scientists are profoundly reluctant to recognize evidence or
contradictions which challenge these basic assumptions. But
paradigms do break down, as latent contradictions become mani-
fest and anomalies accumulate. The 'normal' progress of science
is disrupted by occasional revolutionary transformations of
scientific thought, which usher in a new paradigm - one, perhaps, already prefigured in the work of the profession's disregarded heretics.

Kuhn's distinction between 'normal' and 'revolutionary' periods
in scientific history has been criticized as exaggerated.[2] The
'paradigm' - and Kuhn has used the word quite loosely - is
arguably always evolving; the periods of transition are not
really as disruptive or obviously different as his interpretation
suggests. Any interpretive scheme which attempts to organize
the flow of events into a sequence of historical periods is open
to the objection that the crucial transformations began long
before a period is said to end and continue long after its suc-
cessor is said to have begun. These objections are all the more
forceful when the notion of a paradigm is transferred from the
precisely articulated, self-contained intellectual universe of a

science to the inconsistent, controversial and variously derived doctrines of social policy. But despite this - and even partly because the arguments of policy are seldom very rigorously set out - the attempt to define a paradigm of social policy helps to bring out the underlying assumptions which, I believe, have dominated the debates, the legitimating arguments and radical rebuttals of the past twenty to thirty years. The collapse of this set of assumptions creates the bewilderment of meaning and action which this book set out to explore, disorienting the critical arguments and strategies of the opposition it provoked, as well as the policies it shaped. In this chapter I want to explore what new paradigms of social action may emerge from this bewilderment, especially from the point of view of the actors with which this book has been most concerned. But to understand what can no longer be taken for granted, let me first review the crucial assumptions of the liberal paradigm and why they have lost their hold.

Above all, the paradigm assumed that economic and social relationships could be treated like the relationships of physical sciences. They were regular, lawful, and once understood and respected, could be used to work out the best possible solution to every social problem. Government, therefore, was - or ought to be - largely a matter of applied social science, mediating between the values articulated through the political process and the analysis of the situations in which these values were to be realized. But the values themselves were not arbitrary. Unless the principles of scientific method were followed, good government was impossible: so the values of objectivity, of respect for evidence, of openness of enquiry were beyond question. Ideology, because it implied the manipulation or suppression of evidence in the interests of preconceived beliefs, was to be mistrusted. The paradigm therefore required some non-ideological principle for generating values, capable of guiding rationally the whole enterprise of society.

That principle could only be some formulation of social equality, as a procedure for summing up and legitimating choices. Any assertion of inequality between people that is not based on evidence is itself ideologically prejudiced and therefore irrational. Equality, in this sense, is simply the absence of any a priori principle of differentiation. But, second, the treatment of human relationships in the manner of natural sciences requires that they be reducible to undifferentiated elements which are equivalent and can be substituted one for another. That is, any two atoms of hydrogen combined with any one of oxygen make water; any given number of units of demand for some good, matched to any given number of units of supply make a price. The rich man's penny and the poor man's penny are worth as much in the market. Generalizable laws of human behaviour of these kinds depend on the assumption that individuals behaviours can be reduced to equivalent

units, which can substitute for each other, and whose consequences can be aggregated. The liberal paradigm, therefore,
was inevitably drawn towards some version of the utilitarian
conception of value by its equation of rationality with the
method of natural science. The purpose of government was the
greatest good of the greatest number, where each member of
society represented one unit - or, as Derek Morrell put it at
the Ditchley conference, to maximize the total supply of welfare
and distribute it equitably.

The philosophical difficulties of utilitarianism are notorious,
but so long as gross inequalities of gender, race and class
persist, and cause evident suffering, the logical problems of
defining and summing up units of well-being in any theoretically satisfactory way do not matter very much. Pragmatically,
the paradigm took for granted that the essential goal was to
enhance the well-being of everybody in society - not equally,
because that would upset the incentives on which the maximization of resources depended, but at least in equal proportion,
and if possible in proportions which reduced the differences
in the long run.

Third, the paradigm assumed that, given an understanding
of economic and social laws, and a sense of collective social
purposes, the government of society had the power to use this
knowledge. Essentially, there were two kinds of problems -
cycles of boom and slump, which were to be corrected by
applying Keynesian economic theory; and persistent poverty,
which was to be abolished by a deliberate redistribution of
resources into compensatory benefits and remedial services,
informed by social and psychological research. The crux of
government policy was therefore the continual adjustment of
taxation and public spending, which at once counteracted economic fluctuations by manipulating levels of profit and demand,
and determined the resources available for redistribution. Political and intellectual controversy centred on what balance
between growth and redistribution would maximize the well-
being of everyone in the long run.

A paradigm is not an account of how things are or ought to
be, but a set of working assumptions, to be refined and streng-
thened in use. Those who accepted the paradigm did not have
to claim that governments were consistently rational and competent, or impartially concerned with social equity, or that
economic and social science could solve every problem; but only
that the most progress could be made by acting as if this were
so. The extent to which the principles could ultimately be realized would emerge from practice as a growing body of sophisticated social theory.

This paradigm has until very recently been the predominant
influence upon the way in which domestic policy was conceived
in Western Europe and the United States, and it fundamentally
has a good deal in common with its great historic rival. The
socialist paradigm also tended to represent government as the

highly centralized, expert application of scientific social theory
to maximize economic growth in the interests of society as a
whole, and raised similar issues of the equitable balance between
growth and distribution. Either version sets out a clearly articulated and powerful relationship between theory and action.

In the preceding chapters I have tried to show how, in the
setting of British inner city policies, this liberal paradigm began
to disintegrate. Like any paradigm, its basic assumptions were
flawed by latent inconsistencies, which could be ignored only
so long as the paradigm as a whole seemed to work successfully
– and for twenty years the most highly developed industrial
democracies grew more and more prosperous, enlarged the
scope of social welfare and legislated to enhance equality, confidently elaborating the techniques and professions of rational
problem-solving. But Britain now confronts characteristic problems which neither it nor any other nation knows how to solve
– persistent inflation with rising unemployment, declining investment with growing regional imbalances and the exhaustion of
cheap energy. As the promise of the paradigm fades, the intellectual and moral confidence that upheld its essential principles
begins to falter, and their fragility is exposed.

Looking back, the assumption that governments had (or could
find) the ability to regulate market economies so as to ensure
stability and social equity seems plausible only for a brief span
of history. Britain and the United States emerged from the
Second World War with governments experienced in managing
a wartime economy – directing labour resources, rationing
supplies, planning production and controlling trade. These
governments were much more powerful than any economic organization: they commanded more resources, had far greater scope
of operations and sweeping powers of regulation. The recovery
of the ruined European and Japanese economies depended, in
the first instance, on the resources supplied by the United
States government. Britain was still the centre of an imperial
system of preferential trade. The question, therefore, was not
whether governments had the power to regulate the economy,
domestically and internationally, but how much they should
intervene, to achieve the most efficient and equitable outcome.
Over the next twenty years, the balance of power between
government and corporate control over the economy changed
radically. The extent of direct government control shrank, as
wartime regulations were dismantled and imperial systems liber-
alized. And, as I discussed in chapter 5, although government
expenditure and employment grew, this tended ultimately to
lock governments into a set of commitments which were increasingly difficult to sustain, so that they became more and more
dependent on borrowing from sources controlled and regulated
by international financiers. By contrast, private corporations
grew spectacularly, until a few hundred giants, each wealthier
than many nations, came to dominate the economy of the whole
non-communist world – with an autonomy of control and global

reach no government could match. Instead of government regulating the economy in the interests of overriding social purposes, the economy now seemed to regulate government, in the
interests of profit – which, of course, is what radical critics of
the liberal paradigm had claimed all along.

The paradigm's conception of government was always deeply
ambivalent. In practice – in advising administrations, proposing
and evaluating policies, in the recommendations of public com-
missions – government was treated as an essentially impartial
system, open to the best advice: an instrument for applying
knowledge in the service of society. But in theory government
was itself a subset of the social relationships whose laws the
social sciences set out to discover. It was inconsistent to treat
economic and other social relationships as displaying inherent,
fundamental regularities of behaviour which any rational plan
of intervention needed to understand and respect, yet to treat
government as a disembodied exercise in impartial problem-
solving. Politics was as much open to the investigation of its
natural laws as any other kind of social relationship. Looked
at in this way, political behaviour could be shown to follow its
own logic, where the immediate competition to get and keep
power tended to override any other consideration. Politicians
sacrificed long-term social needs for the sake of present advantages, bureaucracies refused to collaborate in the solution of
mutual problems for fear of losing their autonomy, knowledge
was suppressed or distorted to protect the reputation of unsuc-
cessful policies. In short, against the standard of liberal ideals,
the performance of government was nearly always lamentably
irrational. Yet it was impossible to accept the idea that politics
might be systematically incapable of responding rationally to
the needs of society, without undermining the whole framework
within which meaning and action were integrated.

Again and again, critical analyses – as, for instance, in the
work of Richard Titmuss, Brian Abel-Smith, Peter Townsend,
in Britain, or of Bernard Frieden and Marshal Kaplan, or Martin
Rein and I in the United States[3] – demonstrated how social
policies had failed, and often how they had become distorted
or corrupted by class interests, bureaucratic resistence or
political self-serving. Yet these insights could not be translated into political theory without destroying the context in
which such critical work could be treated as valuable advice.
The liberal paradigm could not generate an applied political
science, in the same sense that it encouraged applied economics
and sociology, because such a science would have been an
illegitimate, Machiavellian intrusion into the ideal of impartial,
rational government. So, despite their critical insight, the
works I have cited tend to end on a note of moral exhortation –
as if, after all, government could transcend politics, once
people's consciences were aroused to the shortcomings of their
society's achievements.

If idealistic social actors become disillusioned with this role of critic and moral guide, they risk falling into extreme self-contempt. The most plausible reconciliation of the inherent inconsistencies in liberal assumptions about government draws an analogy with the relationships of a market economy, as liberal theory conceived of them. Of course, political behaviour is self-interested; but just as the rationally self-interested economic actor helps to ensure the best use of resources through the working of the market, so the democratic free-for-all produces, in the long run, the fairest possible reconciliation of the interests of everyone. The political system can then be both subjected to the methods of science and upheld as an ultimately rational form of government. But this reformulation displaces the ambiguity on to the applied social scientist, whose own assumed role of impartial rationality and moral integrity now has no counterpart in the political system. Experts have little choice but to hire themselves out to partisan political actors – a candidate, a political party, an agency of government, mayor or minister – if they want to influence policy directly. So it is easy to see how expert translates into advocate, and the moral integrity of applied social science comes to depend on its choice of client. The idealistic social critic becomes an advocate for the disadvantaged. The analogy to judicial procedure suggests how partisanship is to be reconciled with a fundamental loyalty to a just and truthful resolution of social conflict. The idea of advocacy therefore became very attractive as a moral justification for the political influence of expertise. It reconciled the contradictory claims of science and commitment, in a context of class interest much easier to define and defend than some consensual notion of the best interest of society as a whole.

But advocacy restores a workable conception of the relationship between knowledge and social action only so long as it stands a fair chance of success. The question is not only whether the political system is capable of representing a fair resolution of class interests, but whether, even if it can, it has the power to carry out the policies which result. If government is, in fact, impotent, the implication is more devastating for advocacy than evidence of systematic class bias, since even a biased system cannot legitimately ignore advocacy which exploits the state's own ideological principles. The Community Development Project teams became disillusioned with advocacy, despite some success in improving plans and services for the communities they served, because government seemed unable to influence in any substantial way the economic disruption at the heart of all their problems. In these circumstances, advocacy for the disadvantaged becomes hypocritical, because it misleads them into wasting their hopes and energies on plans and policies which lead nowhere. As Frances Fox Piven asked in a famous essay, whom does the advocate planner really serve by encouraging disadvantaged communities to turn their energies towards planning?[4] The idealists who try to use their professional expertise to help the poor begin to seem their own worst

enemies - unwitting agents of co-optation and repression. By
the late 1960s, a mood of profound self-doubt, if not self-hatred,
had spread amongst the rising generation of professionals who
were heirs to the liberal tradition.

Advocacy, therefore, leads to demands for the reassertion
of social control over the economy - demands to which government cannot respond within the framework of its own ideology.
The reintegration of expertise with political action - the usefulness of social understanding - seems then to depend on some
radical change in the political system. Applied social science
becomes revolutionary, without necessarily changing its ideals,
or adopting unambiguously any new paradigms of the relationship between knowledge and action.

The evolution of the Community Development Project and the
Docklands plan represent a more complex and subtle intellectual
history than the straightforward refutation of a few very broad
assumptions. But their sequence of conceptions, reformulations
and frustrations reflects the disintegration of this underlying
paradigm, which had dominated social and economic policy for
a quarter of a century, and for a while brought social science
and government together in a way which seemed to make better
intellectual and moral sense. I do not believe that the paradigm
can now be reconstituted, from whatever standpoint of class
or interest we try to understand the context of social action:
not only because the scale and concentration of economic organization is so much greater and less constrained than any
organization of government, but because the latent inconsistencies exposed by this disparity are fundamental. If applied
social science is the model of morally purposeful societal rationality, then the evidence of that science itself shows that the
actual competition for power and resources must distort or
frustrate it. The model is unrealizable.

But the dissolution of a paradigm is not, even in the history
of science, a clear-cut event. Without an agreed new set of
principles to turn to, people continue to act on the old, though
they only half heartedly believe them. Governments still apply
economic theory as if they possessed the capacity to regulate -
even while the president of the United States, in a prepared
television address, admits that neither he nor his advisors
understand the causes of inflation, and doubts whether, in any
case, government could do much about them. Social scientists
are still employed to advise, evaluate, testify, and plan, as if
they contributed an impartial rationality to the determination
of policy - even though most would now admit that the appearance of impartiality only disguises the ideological assumptions
that underlay the relevance of any analysis. Serious journalists
still write as if democratic politics ought to converge upon
relevant, consensual solutions to national problems - while their
own papers describe how the self-interest of powerful groups
constrains and enfeebles consensual policies. Habitual conventions of meaning persist, without conviction, in a jaded re-

enactment of once vital ideas. This bewildering emptiness can go on for a long time, before some favourable conjunction of ideas and events opens the way for a new paradigm to become intellectually and institutionally dominant.

Social policy, unlike science, is not primarily a matter of evidence and interpretation. The disintegration of a paradigm is a crisis only for those few, intellectual actors whose position in the structure of social relationships is disrupted by the collapse of general ideas. Most people define their work socially by the particular function they perform - doctor, fitter, nurse, mother - or by their relationship to the structures of power which determine their parameters of decision. These definitions are, characteristically, far more stable than the ideologies and agencies of policy. Nor do the changes which lead to an intellectual crisis for social policy necessarily result, at the same time, in a political or economic crisis. People can deal with the strains of continual inflation, high unemployment and economic decline, at least for a time, without having to resolve the contradictions and failures of public policy, so long as they can sustain the purposes which give their own lives meaning. Conversely, the ideological revolution that follows a political crisis is responding first of all to the need to justify new constellations of power, not to intellectual issues. Unlike scientific revolutions, new ideological formulations do not necessarily have to incorporate the insights of the old: they may be crude, obscurantist and repressive of obvious truths. So although we can isolate the paradigms inherent in social policy, and trace their evolution through discoveries of knowledge, peer pressure and institutional forms, much as we can trace the evolution of a science, the analogy breaks down if we try to conceive of social and scientific revolutions in the same terms.

Yet the paradigms which underlie policy are still important. A dominant paradigm represents the collective intelligence of society - the ability to ground action on a coherent sense of purpose and bring all relevant knowledge to bear on an issue. Once it disintegrates, policies become more impulsive, opportunistic and vulnerable to intellectual or ideological fads - and being less coherent or consistent, are likely to be cumulatively less successful, on their own terms, and to teach less by their failures. The reintegration of meaning and action concerns everyone eventually, though it concerns most immediately only a small group of intellectual mediators, whose role depends upon it. So although it would be unrealistic to treat the history of social policy as if it were predictable in terms of the emergence and solution of intellectual problems, the potential intellectual grasp of the new paradigms competing for hegemony is as much worth considering as the immediate interests these paradigms represent.

The rest of this chapter, therefore, looks at two emerging conceptions of policy and social action, as if they could be treated purely as paradigms, to be judged by their ability to realize a coherent sense of social purpose in an intelligent, practicable strategy. Since this critique is abstracted from the more complex politics of any actual ideological and social transformation, it cannot foretell what is likely to happen, or even what should happen: but it can show something about the possibilities of reintegrating meaning and action, and what each implies.

In the transformations of science, a revolutionary paradigm not only resolves the anomalies and contradictions which overwhelmed its predecessor, but subsumes all the knowledge previously gained within a more powerful theoretical order. A new paradigm of policy, unlike a merely reactionary political ideology, would not repudiate knowledge because it was acquired within a framework of assumptions since discredited. On the contrary, it would seek to make that knowledge part of a more progressive system of thought, by connecting it with a different set of theoretical relationships. Instead of dismissing 'bourgeois' or 'Marxist' sociology as irrelevant, for instance, the paradigm would need to incorporate the empirically validated discoveries of both traditions; instead of dismissing 'liberal' values, it would incorporate the moral insights of that long and complex struggle with ethical rationality. A new paradigm of social policy would have to take into account everything we have learned, through the practice of democracy and industrial capitalism, about equality and class conflict, freedom and social justice, ideological co-optation and the behaviour of bureaucratic institutions, and everything we have learned, through applying economics, sociology and psychology, about the insights and limits of social science. At the same time, it would resolve the crucial contradiction of liberal policies – that they presuppose a conception of government which has broken down in practice and seems, even in principle, self-contradicting.

From the point of view of the most powerful corporations, the problems of liberalism can be overcome by borrowing a Marxist principle and accepting the social relations of production as paramount. Instead of assuming, like the liberal paradigm, that government regulates economic activity in conformity with social ideals, the new corporate paradigm starts with the opposite assumption – that government must regulate social expectations in accordance with the requirements of the economy. The moral mistake of liberal policy was to set social goals which were incompatible with the incentives to which economic relationships respond, so raising unrealistic expectations, overtaxing and overburdening the economy with a level of social benefits and egalitarian idealism which it could not sustain. The outcome is inflation and economic stagnation, further reducing the ability of government to satisfy expectations. First of all, then, government must find the courage to repudiate these false promises and bring public expenditures and business taxes down to a level compatible with a reinvigorated economy; and to do that, it requires the strong nerves to let at least some of

the voters whose support it suffer. Because it assumes the
subordination of government to economic circumstance, the
paradigm enables policy to treat social hardship with a moral
ruthlessness akin to the philosophy of the poor law reformers
of the nineteenth century: as poor relief bred poverty, so
the sentimental response to economic hardship breeds more
hardship in the long run. The state is not - as liberals had
misguidedly idealized it - a magisterial arbiter between economic and social needs, between the growth of prosperity and its
equitable distribution, but an entrepreneur, trying to make the
most of its country's chances in a competitive international
market. 'Government becomes big business', as John Benington
put it, attacking the ethos of Coventry corporation; not in
the Communist Manifesto's sense of an executive committee of
the capitalist class, but as the manager of a social enterprise
whose viability depends on successfully marketing its assets.
The primary task of government, at every level, is to make the
most of the land, labour, skills, raw materials, infrastructures
and social amenities within its jurisdiction, and ensure that
they are priced to attract the largest possible share of internationally mobile capital. It must therefore manipulate taxes,
environmental controls, subsidies, social and infrastructural
investments, to sustain or restore the competitiveness of the
territory over which it presides, and at the same time discipline
its people to demand no more for themselves than the state of
trade allows.

The British government's recent proposal to solve the problems of the Docklands and other economically declining communities, by creating 'free enterprise zones' with the minimum
of taxation or regulation of any kind, is an extreme, but logical
expression of this paradigm: and the Conservative administration of Margaret Thatcher seems to reflect, beyond its adherence
to monetarism, the more fundamental guidance of these principles.

But they also underlie, for instance, the development policies
of many Southern cities of the United States over the past
twenty years, and of the financial consortium which reconstituted New York City government after its fiscal collapse. As the
American economy weakens, these conceptions emerge more and
more explicitly in the arguments of national policy too. In a
penetrating critique of this 'Recapitalization of Capital', as he
calls it, S.M. Miller traces the ideological ramifications of the
paradigm in recent academic and political debate - a return to
a ruthlessness towards labour, a scepticism towards the claims
of equality, an elitism and repudiation of governmental responsibility for the relief of hardship, which recalls the harshness
of Victorian economic doctrine.[5]

But the new paradigm is not a reactionary revival of nineteenth-century capitalist philosophy. It involves no particular
assumptions about the sovereignty of the market, or the naturally benign outcome of economic competition. It draws on

organizational rather than economic doctrines. The largest
economic organizations have proved to be the most successful,
because their concentrated control over great resources in many
countries enables them to plan more securely, invest on a larger
scale, and adapt more flexibly to disturbances in their environment than any other, and so their predominance increases. They
are not necessarily, by other standards, the most efficient, but
their position is so commanding that everyone's prosperity comes
to depend, directly or indirectly, on the fate of these giants.
Since the aim of the multi-national corporation is assumed to be
the maximization of its profits over the long term, it can be
relied on to deploy its investments around the world so as to
achieve a planned, phased extraction of resources, and a progressive homogenization of standards of living, as production
is directed towards places where labour is cheaper; and the
growing prosperity of these communities, newly incorporated
into the international labour market, generates an expanding
market for goods. This is the multi-national corporate executive's vision of 'a global shopping centre',[6] unencumbered by
the obsolete constraints of nationalism. In principle, even if all
the corporate giants merged into a single monopoly, it would
continue to function in much the same fashion, so long as the
maximization of return from investment remained its guiding rule.

In this corporate world, economic and social theory become
less valuable than organizational experience. If economic
behaviour is determined by a small group of very powerful
actors, theories designed to predict the collective outcome of
millions of independent transactions are no longer needed. The
intelligence of government, therefore, is likely to depend
above all on how well it understands corporate behaviours,
the thinking and information on which it is based. At the same
time, paradoxically, government is likely to become more directly
concerned with relatively small businesses, because these, with
government itself, provide by far the largest proportion of all
employment, and are individually more malleable, by the incentives of planning, towards social ends. From the corporate point
of view, this mass of smaller enterprises provides a correspondingly malleable, dependent economic environment, protecting its
own structure from disturbance. The balance of social and corporate interests, therefore, works itself out through the pattern
in which this subordinate economic structure is deployed.

The paradigm assumes, then, that there is a dominant structure of economic organization to which societies must adapt
themselves, competitively; that social goals incompatible with
competitive success are unrealistic and self-defeating; but intelligent planning in conformity with the logic of the international
organization of capital makes the most of a country's assets. If
every political jurisdiction acts in this way, without inhibiting
the competitive deployment of capital, the growth of global
wealth will be as great and its distribution as fair as possible.

I do not believe that such a paradigm can be dismissed,

simply on the grounds that most people would consider it an unacceptable basis of their country's social policies. In many ways, they have accepted it already: people grumble at multi-national corporations, but they are more likely to blame unemployment and economic decline on their own, or their government's inadequacies, very much as the paradigm encourages them to do. The tradition of democratic party politics itself artificially concentrates debate on the shortcomings of government. Nor does contemporary capitalism naturally generate the kind of class solidarity which Marx foresaw. The hardships it causes are no longer a common experience of long hours and exploitative wages, but a selective deprivation, leaving some without hope of work, others in depressed, marginal employment, but others again - especially in the expanding, capital intensive sectors of the economy - well paid in tolerable working conditions. By contrast, the leading sectors of the nineteenth-century industrial economy, like the cotton mills, were the harshest exploiters of labour. International capitalism sets region against region, nation against nation, the interests of the well-paid, relatively secure worker against the unemployed or marginal one. The trade union, as an organization created to fight the exploitation of workers on the job, is not adapted by its traditions to deal with these issues of selective deprivation and insecurity, and risks protecting the more privileged workers at the expense of the rest. So the new economic order does not generate, spontaneously, a growing solidarity of working-class opposition, but fragments it. And since it works largely within the same institutional framework as liberal policies it displaces, it disguises how radically it has transformed the commitment to universal social protection.

I do not mean to imply that no broad movement of protest against such policies is likely to arise: I want to discuss later, in the context of a different conception of the future, how this might happen. For the present, I want only to suggest that the paradigm is not obviously self-contradictory: it would not necessarily provoke its own overthrow, so long as it delivers the goods and therefore could, I believe, become - at least for a political, administrative and intellectual elite - the accepted paradigm on which to base the policies of democratic government.

But the goods it would have to deliver imply an extraordinary power to sustain growth, if enough people are still to believe that they will gain most from adapting to the needs of this kind of economic management. What if the resources of the earth cannot provide the means for such growth, or human life survive the consequences?

This question is one starting point of an alternative paradigm, whose essential principles emerge from the convergence of movements which set out from many different concerns. It assumes that continual economic growth is impossible, even if human societies could withstand indefinitely the scale of changes it imposed, because the fossil fuels on which it has depended will

sooner or later be exhausted; and before then, the use of
energy at such a rate is likely to cause irreparable damage
to the natural world which sustains human life. So it replaces
the ideal of growth with an ecological ideal of balance. Human
society has to embody a self-renewing cycle of activity: otherwise it is constantly exhausting the capacity of its level of
exploitation, and so either collapses, or transforms itself into
a more powerfully exploitative system. Each transformation leads
towards a more devastating final collapse, because the exhaustion is more complete. Entrepreneurial capitalism, since it sustains itself by just such constant transformations in the exploitation of resources is, therefore, increasingly destructive. Both
the incentives and techniques of its productive system have
to be redesigned to reduce, progressively, the rate at which
unrenewable resources are being exhausted, and unusable waste
discharged.

This requires much broader social control of economic decisions, not only to take care of resources and prevent pollution,
but to tackle all the social tensions and inequalities which cannot any longer be palliated by promised increases in general
prosperity. Poverty and unemployment have to be remedied by
reforming the way in which resources are used rather than by
enlarging the sum of distributable wealth. But the form of
control would be very different from the centralized management
of most socialist nations, which has been directed towards indus-
trailization and more intensive exploitation of resources, or
from the bureaucratic regulation of capitalist nations, which
tries only to circumscribe autonomous economic activity. From
an ecological point of view, chains of exchange between people
and their habitat are crucial: and these will breakdown in
periodic disasters unless the exchanges between people themselves are also mutually sustaining.

This ecological way of seeing brings out aspects of social and
political rights which the liberal paradigm neglected. Instead of
thinking about social justice only in terms of the equal treatment
of equivalent units, it acknowledges the right of each community
of people to a familiar habitat, like creatures in the natural
world. It recognizes the attachments which bind people to each
other and to places, and out of which evolve the unique meaning of each person's life. Social policies cannot therefore be
decided by aggregating needs, abstracted from a particular
context. They are an integral part of the way work, production,
services are co-ordinated to meet everyone's needs, in complex
patterns of interaction which vary from place to place. If these
patterns of exchange are to be managed fairly and knowledge-
ably, without bureaucratic clumsiness, their control must be
socially inclusive, widely dispersed and embodied in the way in
which people handle the transactions of everyday life. So in
place of the liberal ideal of government as a rational and
impartial arbiter of the public interest, reconciling accumulation
with justice, the paradigm reintegrates government with the

co-operative management of everyday life, as a pervasive,
decentralized process of mutual accommodation.

Correspondingly, social analysis has to be directed towards
understanding complex patterns of inter-relationship more than
to discriminating and isolating factors. To know that a particular
factor accounts for a substantial proportion of the variance is
useful, if you want to intervene in an external set of relationships to change the outcome. Both the regulative tasks of
liberal economic policy and the compensatory tasks of liberal
social policy are characteristically conceived of in this way.
This is consistent with their conception of social rights as
individual rights of access to generalizable benefits – such as
decent accommodation, health care, a minimum of income. The
questions for analysis then typically concern the amount of
unmet need and what proportion of it a proposed intervention
might make good. But once these questions of provision are
seen in the context of a largely self-governing community, the
analysis of need becomes, itself, part of a discussion in which
everyone concerned should have the right to join. The needs
are no longer abstract and generalizable, but in a particular
place, and caught up in a particular pattern. So the paradigm
implies a conception of social research more akin to the methods
of social anthropology, but less detached, where the process
of learning is a reciprocal mutual endeavour of observer and
observed.

This sense of a new paradigm, though it is still blurred by
ambiguities, represents the convergence of several distinct
movements and campaigns. The environmental movement, as a
response to the destruction of wilderness and natural species,
merges into a more general concern with devastation and pollution; and since these issues – at least in highly developed,
industrial societies – are so closely connected to the extracting
and burning of fossil fuels, they lead into questions of energy
conservation and use. These in turn involve control over energy
production, and the implications of nuclear power, as the succeeding technology – the huge capital investments, highly
centralized control and terrifying risks. The search for less
dangerous, costly or polluting alternatives to either nuclear
power or more exhaustive mining of coal and oil – such as solar
energy and conservation – becomes, then, partly a reaction
against centralized, high technology means of energy production.
It leads towards advocating decentralized, relatively cheap,
environmentally sensitive and resource-conserving energy
policies under local control. Since energy is crucial to all human
activity, this effectively implies the principles of the paradigm
I have sketched.

These arguments and movements, which start from fear of the
physical consequences of technology, converge with those
which began as a reaction against the social consequences of
advanced technologies in less developed countries, and then
turned to apply the same arguments to the technologically

advanced countries themselves - in E.F. Schumacher's work on appropriate technology, for instance, or in Ivan Illich's critiques of modern medicine and the technical elaboration of industrial society.[7] As its scale and rate increase, the concentration of power and remoteness of control inherent in the development of more and more sophisticated technologies begins to seem as socially disruptive and unmanageable for highly industrialized countries as for poorer, rural societies undergoing an earlier stage of modernization. So, like the environmental critique, the social critique of technology comes to emphasize principles of decentralization and social control over economic development.

The experience of community action and development, in both Britain and the United States, leads towards a similar ideal of how social and economic policy should be reconstituted. The Coventry Workshop, for instance, set out to bring community groups and organized workers together in a campaign to assert a much stronger community influence over economic investment, eventually drawing local government to their side. American industrial cities which, like Coventry, face the prospect of severe decline and disinvestment, are beginning to look for the same kind of alliance between workers, community and city government to restore their economic base. Movements such as the Campaign for Economic Democracy in the United States reflect this resistance to the disruption of local economies by remote corporations preoccupied with the rationalization of their investments.[8]

But the idea of community control also grows out of a thirty-year history of opposition to slum clearance and urban renewal, which has continually sought to explain and defend the vitality and uniqueness of the familiar patterns of relationship inherent in places. And in the United States, especially, this opposition has often been, at the same time, an assertion of racial identity and autonomy in the face of a dominant culture which seemed to offer equality, even in principle, only at the price of expropriation. Both have helped to establish community rights to take part in planning and to act as the agent of its own development.

All these arguments, movements and campaigns, stemming from issues of environmental protection, of energy and nuclear power, of development in Africa, Asia and Latin America, of community development and ethnic identity, of industrial decline and economic revival, share a common hostility to highly concentrated, remote, hierarchical forms of economic management, independent of social responsibilities and social ties; and a common mistrust of the science this style of management induces. The principles they emphasize in reaction - social responsibility against economic autonomy; decentralized, democratic control against remote, concentrated, corporate hierarchies of control; understanding the whole against the abstraction of partial relationships - become the elements of the emerging paradigm whose form I have tried to interpret.

There are other influences, too: some more profound, if less direct. In a predominantly masculine culture of specialized careers and almost fanatically single-minded images of success, women have been left the task of healing fragmented lives: and because women have been more deeply concerned than men with the relationships between family, community, the exploitation of labour and the pressure of career, they have been the driving force behind most community action, the most insightful critics of the capitalist culture of work. So women's movements often identify the same enemies and put forward similar ideals of social reintegration.

A paradigm of policy, in the sense in which I have used the phrase in this chapter, is a set of principles, articulating a relationship between social purposes, government and learning, as a scientific paradigm articulates the relationship between question, method and finding. Many different kinds of movement seem to converge to form more or less explicitly, in this sense, the principles of a paradigm; and sketchy as it is, it has provided a framework within which much political action has set its meaning, as an alternative social ideal to the recapitalization – or reindustrialization – of capital. Like a scientific paradigm, its assumptions define the new problems, and the method for arriving at their solution. It is not a statement of policy, or a complete prescription: it does not explain, for instance, how local social control of the economy is to be integrated in any larger system, or how intractable conflicts of interest are to be reconciled. Like its liberal predecessor or its corporate rival, it represents something less definite than a theory or an ideology, but in some ways more influential – a consistent bias towards certain principles of thought and action, which reinforce each other.

But its principles presuppose a much more radical transformation of power than does the international economic and social order proposed by the alternative paradigm, whose assumptions it contradicts. Without an idea of how this transformation can be brought about, the paradigm does not represent a real alternative, and activity it inspires will not mean much in the end. The integration of meaning and action depends on being able to see how changes can be made to happen, as well as knowing what they are for. But these two kinds of knowledge are not necessarily – or perhaps even usually – compatible. The analysis of social structures, which represents most powerfully the need for radical changes, because it shows how what is wrong is integrated in the whole system of relationships, can be paradoxically self-defeating. It is characteristically biased towards metaphors which cannot themselves accommodate processes of change.

The next chapter takes up this question.

6 METAPHORS

Each of the paradigms of policy discussed in the last chapter integrates its distinctive concerns with ideas of government and knowledge fundamentally different from the others: and so each would put the effective exercise of power in different hands – public administrators and their expert advisors; corporate executives and their political counterparts; representatives of community interests and needs. Looked at in this way, the transformation of social policy, as a shift in paradigm, involves a corresponding transformation in who holds power and how it is institutionalized. Conversely, whatever reinforces the existing structure of power inhibits transformation.

The members of the Community Development Project, as they were led towards a more radical analysis, tended to see community action in this light: and so they confronted a dilemma which characteristically troubles all practically minded radical movements. The more successfully they work within the existing structure of opportunity to achieve steps towards their ultimate ideals, the more they seem to extend the adaptability and responsiveness of that structure, and so put any deeper transformation farther off; but if they refuse to work within this structure, they are usually left with very few choices – education and propaganda, forming their own communities, demonstrating and protesting – which generally seem marginal, isolated or abortive. This dilemma, as a choice between co-optation and marginality, recurs again and again, in disguised or open form, in discussions of strategy. It is also, particularly for people who work in social services, often a moral dilemma: how can one not try to make things work better for people, even if this involves using and defending an institutional structure with which one is at heart disillusioned?[1]

Yet, despite all the experiences which seem to confirm it, the dilemma is partly an artificial consequence of the way in which power is conceived of; a logical inference from the way relationships are represented, rather than a necessary condition of action. Every analysis is informed by some metaphor – clockwork, waves, currents, building – through which its relationships become imaginatively graspable. The metaphor implies the kinds of action which are possible or impossible by that analogy; and so, irrespective of its ability to represent reality, one metaphor may inhibit or encourage action more than another. In this chapter, I discuss two ways of thinking about social change, each deriving from a different metaphor, which respectively reinforce the dilemma and dissolve it. I hope the discussion will help to show in what sense incremental actions can lead towards social transformation, and what justifies pragmatic attempts to change things for the better, even when they do not change enough.

The metaphor which came to dominate the understanding of inner city problems was structure. The British government increasingly talked of structural problems and the need for structural planning: the reports of the Community Development Project write of the structure of contemporary capitalism. This structural metaphor was introduced from the Left, and insisted upon, because it represented the interconnections between neighbourhood, city, nation and the international economy as an indivisible set of relationships. The Community Development Project teams, and the Docklands Action Groups, wanted to demonstrate these connections, so as to impel government to intervene on behalf of impoverished neighbourhoods at the highest level of control of which it was capable - to show that neighbourhood problems could only be solved by a national or even international strategy for controlling the process of capital-accumulation. For that purpose, the structural metaphor was forceful and persuasive: the government's White Paper on inner city policy, in adopting the language of structure, also necessarily accepted a larger and more direct responsibility for what was happening.

Most literally, the metaphor implied that cracks in the social fabric, the decay of neighbourhoods, could not be made good by repairs where the damage showed, but involved rebuilding the structure of society; that apparent social problems were signs of underlying tensions and distortions whose consequences, if they were superficially patched or cobbled in one place, would only break out elsewhere. It challenged, specifically, the earlier metaphor of a poverty cycle, where disadvantages grew and reseeded themselves in a self-perpetuating culture. To see a structure redirected attention from the community with its 'tangle of pathologies' to the foundations on which its misfortunes were built.

A structure, as a way of imaging relationships, represents events which occur sequentially as if they were simultaneous. A complex set of relationships and the interactions amongst them can then be seen as a whole, as if everything were happening at once. So, for instance, an organizational chart might show a number of labelled boxes, arranged roughly in a pyramid, with lines joining some ones to others, as a characteristic representation of a hierarchical institution. But what is being represented exists only as a sequence of requests, commands, responses which are assumed to reproduce themselves constantly in the static pattern pictured. Similarly, the international organization of production can be seen as a structure branching out from a few centres of command to control resources and materials across the world, directing where accumulated capital is reinvested. In the radical image, this structure also builds up a set of subordinate governmental and ideological relationships. In the final analysis, virtually all relationships of society come to be seen as part of the structure: all labour and resources, whether they are being used or held in reserve, are represented as manipulable to conform to the requirements of the structure. This imagery makes a visible and compelling connection between the abstract dynamics of global capitalism and what an urban neighbourhood is going through.

But the qualities of the metaphor, which make complex relationships of interdependence appear compelling and comprehensible, correspondingly make change harder to conceive of. In structural imagery, because past, present and future have to be represented as simultaneous, relationships are necessarily predetermined. That is, they can only be presented as a structure if they will reproduce themselves predictably in conformity with a pattern: so, by definition, they will suppress any behaviour that would prevent them reproducing themselves. The structure cannot change itself: it can only succumb to attrition. Structural metaphors of social relationships are convincing because our experience of institutions so often seems to confirm this inadaptability: everyone is locked into a pattern of mutual constraint, frustrating any initiative of reform. Change can only come from outside. But if a structural metaphor is applied to society as a whole, who is the external agent?

In the Marxist tradition of social analysis the agent of change is, of course, the working class as a whole, as it grows into self-awareness. But if capitalist relationships can be represented as sustaining themselves by a mutually reinforcing structure of economic, political and ideological control, then the working class appears to be incorporated in that structure, its institutions and ideology manipulated into compatibility with the requirements of capitalism. Combining a dialectic of class struggle with a structural analysis produces an ambiguous conception of the working class as at once inside the capitalist structure, captive, and yet capable of reconstituting itself outside it. This ambiguity tends to make radical strategies seem ineffectual: they set out to help people grasp their position within a capitalist society and organize to change it, but the analysis is so overwhelming in the scope and control of the forces it describes as to make any local, countervailing response seem futile. So long as change is seen in structural terms, any particular change in relationships seems foredoomed to co-optation or suppression unless all other relationships change simultaneously. This implies that very extensive alliances, based on a shared theoretical understanding, have to be established before any substantive changes can be achieved. Until then, radical political actions have to be seen as aspects of the creation of alliances, or as training exercises designed, in the last resort, to heighten awareness. Without concerted reinforcement, any change will be exposed to eventual reincorporation into the

existing system. This conception of political strategy implies
an extraordinary ability to work out in advance the way in
which actions undertaken in a complex, varied and far-reaching
context of relationships will converge. according to an intellectual analysis which is itself constantly under debate. It
tends to discount the impulses which in practice draw people
into political collaboration - the outrage at injustice or exploitation, the shared grievances. Instead, it presents the frustratingly abstract goal of a revolution which is neither presently
achievable nor approachable through incremental gains.

As an heuristic device, therefore, structural metaphors suggest a dauntingly exacting ideal of acting to change society. But
how would the possibilities seem different if the same circumstances - the same forces of capitalism, the same pressures
towards ideological conformity and the same forms of government - were looked at in any other way? Suppose we turn our
attention from the structure of relationships to the way in which
they are reproduced. A structural analysis takes social conformity for granted, as an outcome of the ideological and material
pressures embodied in the social system. But conformity is not
taken for granted in the conduct of everyday life. The reproduction of reliable patterns of relationship is a constant preoccupation, from the rules of conversation to the rule of law.
Manufacturers do not take for granted that the public will buy
their products, or authorities that their orders will be properly
obeyed. The reproduction of social relationships requires continual effort, attention and collaboration in which everyone,
consciously or unconsciously, is involved every day of their
lives. Even in the most casual conversation, for instance, we
follow rules and conventional cues which enable us to take
turns at speaking without either interrupting each other or
leaving awkward pauses; and when someone misses a cue, or
infringes the rules, the conversation characteristically doubles
back to repair the fault. From the momentary failure to respond
with those characteristic facial movements, by which people
show they are listening, from a shift in posture, or a phrase,
we pick up very subtle hints that we have not said quite what
was expected; and in turn we modulate tones of voice, conversational pauses and gestures, to indicate when we are not
satisfied with a response.[2] All this is so necessary a part of
reciprocal behaviour that it becomes second nature to us. We
continually trust each other to observe the rules by which
human exchanges become predictable enough to be manageable.
The disruptiveness of insanity and our fear of it arises - as
Erving Goffman has described so vividly[3] - largely because the
behaviour that we call mad is unresponsive to the limits,
encouragements and rebukes which we use to regularize each
other's behaviours.

Because everyone has to be able to predict behaviour to
manage the relationships of everyday life successfully, there is
a very powerful pervasive impetus to assert familiar categories

of relationship – even when they imply the inevitability of
subservience, injustice or unhappiness. For better or worse,
they are the categories in which we have learned to cope with
the world: and because we need to find meaning in our lives,
we create the arguments for the conformity we have chosen.
Legitimate authority gains its power from this constant, diffuse
reinforcement: so long as we accept the constraints it imposes
on what we can choose, we continually rationalize our accommodation to these constraints as the right thing to do, and
assert this rationality to others. Even those who are most
blatantly victimized by the assumptions of a dominant ideology
tend to accommodate by compensatory behaviour which reinforces their apparent validity – as, for instance, those denied
opportunities teach each other to ridicule ambition. Hence there
is a general predisposition throughout society to keep faith with
its essential legitimating principles, which all authority exploits.
A structural analysis can be restated in these terms as the
processes by which control over resources becomes translated
into all the diffuse constraints regulating social relationships.

But it is very important to recognize that these processes
are neither automatic nor unselfconscious.

In modern, industrial capitalist societies, especially, where
scarcely anyone has a traditional, prescribed place, conformity
is necessarily an act of choosing, even if the choices for most
people seem all to come to much the same in the end. Throughout our lives, we are constantly deciding whose expectations
we will meet. In choosing an occupation, a neighbourhood to
live in, an offer of friendship, we continually define the person
we want to be taken for, and we work hard to be what we have
chosen, to understand what is expected of us and fulfil it.
However constrained these choices are, we rarely perceive
them simply as the inevitable outcome of our situation. On the
contrary, we characteristically feel the need to justify them,
to assert their moral and rational superiority to all the other
ways of being which we have more or less consciously rejected,
to reassure ourselves and convince others that whatever we
have become stands in a good light against the backdrop of
our unrealized selves. We justify even the stress and hardship
our choices entail – as those in hazardous occupations take
pride in the dangers which set them apart.

These rationalizations are too idiosyncratic, subtle and various
to be treated merely as the internalization of a dominant ideology. The countless everyday acts which reproduce social
relationships depend on beliefs which make them meaningful to
each actor in the circumstances of a unique life. Though they
derive from received ideas of moral conduct, they are necessarily personal interpretations adapted to particular situations.
They are scarcely ever automatic reiterations of imposed rules,
but judgments which have to be defended. People give much
thought and energy to criticizing each other's behaviour –
especially the behaviour of those they most immediately depend

upon. Gossip, quarrels, grievances and their adjudication constantly exchange and refine people's perception of behaviour
so as to develop in everyone a capacity for moral intuition partly
independent of any particular set of relationships. In the complex variety of circumstances of modern industrial society,
social conformity itself depends on the ability to establish
principles of behaviour at a level of abstraction high enough to
inform very different kinds of relationship. This need to
generalize, to distinguish the justifying principle from the conventions governing a set of relationships, opens the rightness
of any particular relationships to question, requiring of everyone a capacity to defend the way in which they interpret the
very abstract shared ideals of society in their own lives. People
acquire a habit of reflexive, critical judgment. The members of
complex industrial societies are ideologically self-conscious
because the cohesion of society requires it; but once they
become self-conscious, they can also make moral choices critical
of the relationships within which they are required to act.
  This helps to explain apparently contradictory aspects of
social relationships. The structural representation of society
emphasizes the interlocking, mutually reinforcing constraints
which direct behaviour; and most people, most of the time, do
indeed feel that they are powerless to change society or even
the circumstances of their own lives. Yet we also treat social
behaviours as voluntary. The experience of everyday life is not,
characteristically, of reiterating pre-determined responses -
except in the kind of routine or mass production work which
seems most de-humanizing. We act as if we could have behaved
differently, and so are responsible for what we did. Because
social relationships are being reproduced all the time by countless more or less conscious and deliberate acts of conformity,
to which each of us brings his or her own moral and intellectual
justifications, we are at once constrained by them and yet
responsible for them.
  The reproduction of social relationships depends, then, on
whether people go on believing that they must conform to them.
The power to influence this belief does not lie only in the power
to control the consequences of behaviour, to reward or punish,
but also in the persuasiveness of moral insight. Movements of
social change which, in the first instance, commanded scarcely
any material resources have become powerful through the force
of their moral appeal. Once people see relationships in a light
which leads them to repudiate established conventions of behaviour, all the vast, diffuse social energy that went into meeting expectations, into asserting and justifying conformist
behaviour, is released and open to redirection. Social movements
- trades unionism, women's suffrage, civil rights - characteristically begin to mobilize support through the actions of a few
people foolhardy enough to resist intimidation and withstand
the consequences. They show that it is possible to act differently. What they represent has now to be chosen or rejected.

It cannot any longer be disregarded as unthinkable, and so
they change the assumptions by which everyone has to justify
their actions. The cumulative effect of this demonstration can
be very powerful, as more and more people recognize in it a
moral challenge which they cannot evade.

While the structure of power seems remote and abstract - an
interlocking regulation of vast resources by a few unknown
men in private meetings - the process by which that power is
reproduced is immediately accessible. It exists only so long as
each of us does what is expected of us - buys what we are
supposed to buy, wants what we are supposed to want, votes
for the politicians whose claims are expected to appeal to us,
fears the punishments of nonconformity and values the rewards
of going along. All the great concentrations of economic and
political control are in the last resort only effective so long as
their means of regulating everyday behaviour function as
expected. The structure of power is at bottom a psychological
structure - a set of assumptions, hopes, fears and needs which
the members of society have been induced to incorporate. The
more people refuse inducements, withstand intimidations, question assumptions, demand new kinds of information, repudiate
values or norms of behaviour, the more powers of control are
driven back upon physical coercion: and any authority which
can only reproduce the governing relationships of society by
a constant exercise of force is precarious. It has to pre-empt
so many productive resources merely to assert its control that
it cannot satisfy even its own supporters, redoubles its repres-
siveness, and ends by being unable to command its own army
or police.

From this point of view, the distinction between reform and
radical action no longer seems so absolute. In terms of the
structural metaphor, reforms are essentially repairs - they
replace the rotten beams, reopen jammed doors, shore up sag-
ging supports and refurbish the façade. Radical acts are, by
contrast, essentially destructive - they clear the ground for
a new structure. Anything they seek to create must be independent of the structure they intend to pull down. Any apparent
alliance with reform must be subversive. But in terms of the
reproduction of relationships, reforms as well as radical actions
may be working towards profound and far-reaching changes in
the expectations which govern relationships. In so far as they
share the same ideals, they reinforce each other. So, for
instance, the principles which informed the American civil
rights acts raised expectations which could not be constrained
by the expedient modification of certain racist institutions in
the Southern states. Similarly, once President Johnson had
asserted the eradication of poverty as an expectation of policy,
he could not contain the resonance of that challenge, nor the
movements which it helped to provoke. All changes - even the
most conservative in intent - reformulate the context in which
people make choices about their behaviour, reviving the self-

consciousness of choice, and so have repercussions which
cannot be reliably controlled or predicted. Hence reforms can
help to provoke more radical changes by the way in which they
upset the stability of the assumptions which legitimate society.

But if an analysis in terms of the reproduction of relationships
makes the disruption of existing patterns seem more possible,
and more incremental, it also brings out obstacles to recon-
structing new relationships which a structural analysis ignores.
A structural metaphor suggests that a political movement powerful enough to disrupt the existing structure of relationships
ought to be powerful enough to impose another structure in its
stead. Once it has amassed the critical momentum to knock down,
it should command the resources to rebuild. The power to disrupt and the power to establish relationships appear symmetrical. But often, just when a political movement seems to be
succeeding, it dwindles into insignificance: it becomes lost in
indeterminate reformist endeavours, falls victim to a reactionary
counter-attack, or breaks down in factional disputes. If the
power to build and destroy is symmetrical, then these failures
imply that the power structure was never effectively disrupted
in the first place: in the face of apparent defeat it merely withdrew to regroup its formidable powers of co-optation and repression. This implies that the established order is even more
indomitable and resilient than at first it seemed. So the act of
destruction is, from this point of view, more than ever the
crucial and problematic task, upon which the mobilization of
countervailing resources has to centre. Once that has been
decisively accomplished, the same resources can be diverted
to the task of reconstruction.

But in the account I gave above of the way in which social
relationships are reproduced, the power to disrupt and to
establish relationships are not symmetrical. A given pattern of
relationships will continue only so long as everyone involved
continues to behave as expected. Once people question whether
they are pragmatically or morally bound by these expectations,
the pattern becomes vulnerable: and this questioning is not, I
suggest, readily suppressed by any institutional ideological
control, because the self-justifications which determine whether
in practice, in everyday life, people conform to established
expectations arise out of an idiosyncratic, personal context of
meaning which is largely independent of arguments in the public
domain. The more tightly integrated and far-reaching the
relationships of society, the more disruptive will be a refusal to
conform to expected behaviours in any part of it. But, correspondingly, to establish a new pattern of expectations everyone must be persuaded or coerced into resolving the uncertainties created by disruption in a mutually coherent manner, and
this is obviously very much more difficult to achieve. An organization of resources powerful enough to mobilize effective disruption is not necessarily powerful enough to draw the forces it
has mobilized together in establishing any stable new pattern

of reciprocal expectations. Its failure does not prove that the
preexisting order possessed overwhelming powers of co-optation
or repression: only that people will tend to revert to already
familiar ways of doing things in the absence of any other
principles of behaviour clear and authoritative enough to make
life tolerably predictable. The frustrations of movements to
change society arise, not so much from the entrenched power
of the established order, as from its inherent fragility. Stable,
broadly accepted expectations of relationships are easily disrupted but hard to re-establish in any new form. Hence political movements are constantly being defeated by the incoher-
ence of the expectations they provoke: or their ideals are
perverted by the force called up to coerce a new conformity.

The strategic implications of thinking in these terms are the
opposite of the structural analysis. Instead of concentrating
on the mobilization of ever greater disruptive resources, to
counteract the repressive resilience of the established order,
the hardest and most crucial task is to establish a sense of the
relationships we want to create so clear, so persuasive, and so
mundane that people's behaviour will begin to converge upon
these expectations in all the transactions of everyday life. Only
then are the opportunities created by the spontaneous or contrived disruption of existing relationships exploitable.

Both the civil rights movement and the women's movement
illustrate this principle. Each defines explicitly, in the context
of everyday life, the patterns of expectation which must be
repudiated, and the expectations of equal respect which must
replace them, elaborating codes of language and conduct which
enable non-racist, non-sexist patterns of interaction to emerge.
In the same way, each can specify how law, public policy and
institutional practices must be revised to accommodate these new
conceptions of relationship. This powerful convergence of pressures for new patterns of conformity does not require that either
movement present a unified ideology, nor a single conception
of what an ideal society would be like, nor a single underlying
strategy of change. Conversely, when people do not have a
clear conception of the expectations which, in all the circumstances of everyday affairs, should govern relationships in
place of those they are seeking to disrupt, they will always find
that the initiative is taken from them, just at the moment when
their tactics have been successful enough to open the opportunity.

I have argued that structural metaphors, by their very
nature, make radical changes appear impossible. We seem to
march about the citadel of power, trumpeting our ideals of a
better world, like so many Joshuas waiting for History, or the
People, or Science to smite down its towering battlements. If,
instead, we think in terms of the reproduction of relationships,
rather than their structure, this image of powerlessness
becomes transformed: we make the citadel, we constantly
recreate it, inside ourselves and in our dealings with each

other, and so, surely, we can begin to unmake it. But this way of looking at the problems of change has its own conceptual traps. If the structural metaphor seems to put the actor outside the context of action, with no way to get in, the metaphor of reproduction so centres everything within the actor's experience that there is no way to get out. The connections which we cannot see between one set of actions and another - the unintended effects of our actions, their remote consequences - are not now represented; and so we lose sight of the question of whether what we are doing achieves, in the long run, what we intend.

Despite their achievements, for instance, the effectiveness of the civil rights movement and the women's movement is still far more narrowly circumscribed than either intended. Neither has materially affected poverty or inequality of opportunity either for black people or white women. The proportions of women or minorities admitted to the 5 per cent of privileged positions in society can change substantially without noticeably affecting their disproportionate concentration amongst the 20 per cent who are poor. Both movements, I think, tended to assume that changing specifically discriminatory relationships would provoke changes in the expectations governing all kinds of relationships to which women or minorities would gain access. Black professionals would have a more sympathetic and intimate understanding of black clients, black businessmen would employ black workers to meet the needs of black communities, women would conduct their professional lives without the strident competitiveness of masculine sexual insecurity. But none of these hoped-for consequences was worked out with the clarity and practicality of the attack on discriminating relationships themselves. There was, and is, no well-articulated conception of what the woman executive or black professional should do differently, in the conduct of their careers, from their white male colleagues. For the most part they reinforce the existing expectations of relationships by showing that they can fulfil them as well as anyone. Without a broader understanding of social and economic relationships - of the kind that a structural analysis presents - both movements risk stopping short of the changes which affect the life chances of women and minorities more deeply.

Understanding processes of change and understanding their consequences are not the same. The metaphors which help to portray one kind of understanding can mislead the other, and unless we recognize that these categories of thought are metaphors, not direct representations of reality, with particular uses and limitations, arguments about social change readily become boxed in by the mutually exclusive logic of particular metaphors. As the more radical, structural analysis of inner city problems evolved, it began to inhibit action in this way. It represented the power to control the destiny of society as remote, concentrated and inaccessible to ordinary people; in consequence, local actions which challenged the way in which

things were done were doomed to co-optation or suppression
unless they could be co-ordinated in a comprehensive strategy
for revolution; and therefore reform and radical change were
antithetical. Any effective strategy of social transformation had
to meet a virtually impossible set of conditions. But as I have
tried to show, these are consequences of the metaphor rather
than the analysis it represents. Despite the enormous concentrations of economic power; despite the remoteness of the decisions which determine the fate of a factory or a neighbourhood;
despite the subservience of political institutions to the requirements of capital; despite the ideological manipulation embodied
in control over newspapers and television - despite all this, it
only works because most people, most of the time, choose to
go along with it.

Of course, they do not choose freely. Every child has been
moulded into conformity by love and disapproval, rewards and
punishments. Our adult autonomy is no more than the ability
to see this structure of reward and punishment, in our relationships and in ourselves, with more detachment and a more
independent judgment of the power and validity of its constraints. We are suspicious of exhortations to make moral choices,
because this is how we have been brought up to conform - constantly urged to choose freely what we are being constrained
to accept. Yet learning to exercise an independent judgment
is also, as I suggested earlier, a necessary part of our social
upbringing. In education, in search of a career, getting married, voting, we are supposed to choose for ourselves: and the
legitimacy of those choices, in the ethos of democratic society,
depends on their being neither bought nor coerced. This double-
bind - the requirement to be at once free and conforming -
creates an ideological tension where we constantly accept moral
responsibility for actions which, at the same time, we believe
to be manipulated in ways we cannot control.

But this ambiguous element of choice and independent judgment is crucial to understanding social changes, because it
leads to a basic question of strategy: when are people open to
choosing differently from their habit? Most obviously, when the
rewards and punishments change; when, for instance, inflation
or economic disaster rob the prudent and conforming of their
lifetime's savings; when conscientious and thoughtful voters
find that the people they elected are contemptuous and corrupt;
when behaviour, once repressed, acquires legitimacy or consistently escapes sanctions. And, perhaps even more than in
those circumstances, people have to choose afresh when the
ideological confusion of society, the weakness of government
and unpredictability of events makes it harder to know what
conformity is, or what may be rewarded or punished.

These critical periods of social choice are also stressful; and
under stress people are vulnerable to ideas which displace or
deny the sources of their anxiety. The choices they make in
times of social disintegration, therefore, will not reflect simply

a rational reassessment of their self-interest. People will look for scapegoats, turn towards myths of a homelier past, retreat into other-worldly religions or extreme self-centredness, or into the simple, cathartic meanings of violent conflict - and all these impulses are open to manipulation, as much as the search for a better understanding. So the choices people make will not be spontaneously compatible; their convergence depends upon the way in which their need to choose is guided and exploited. From the point of view of a social movement, therefore, it is crucially important to offer a realizable and attractive ideal of relationships for people to choose.

This perhaps seems obvious. But the most influential tradition of radical change, stemming from Marx, does not really do this. The socialism of the early industrial revolution was based on a vision of the future, and it inspired, especially in America, communities which set out to live by its principles. By contrast Marxism, contemptuous of this 'Utopianism', is uniquely retro-spective. It conceives of the growth of a revolutionary movement as the convergence of people upon the same analysis of existing society, and the same consciousness of a shared class interest. Any movement which requires that its members agree upon a single analysis and a single definition of their social identity implies a much greater degree of conformity than a movement based on the same broad ideals of the future.

The outcome of any social transformation depends on how all the diffuse and centrifugal impulses of a disintegrating order are made to converge in a new order predictable enough to reproduce itself. But as the discussion of paradigms in the last chapter suggested, this coherence does not have to depend on ideological conformity. Different ideologies may converge on corresponding principles of social relationships out of which a new paradigm emerges. As different kinds of movements - social, political, environmental, artistic - recognize this cor-respondence and support each other, the experience of working together begins to define pragmatically what the paradigm is. Because a paradigm represents a set of working principles - assumptions, methods, purposes, by which to learn - it is inherently more open than an ideology as a basis of convergence. It does not assert any particular meaning, only the framework within which any meaning can be validly expressed, and any-thing can properly be said to have been learned. These under-lying principles of convergence can be assimilated with far less invasion of each person's own interpretation of experience than the demands of an ideology.

I suggested in the last chapter that a new social paradigm, like a scientific paradigm, should not only resolve the contra-dictions of its predecessor, but also incorporate its insights. One of the deepest preoccupations of the liberal tradition of social thought we inherit concerns the nature of conformity. Sociology, psychoanalysis, Western Marxism, have all helped to develop a far more sophisticated understanding of the pos-

sibilities and limits of personal autonomy within a social structure than any earlier generations could turn to. Any social
movement that disregarded or repudiated this understanding
would be intellectually regressive as well as politically repressive.

All this leads me to conclude that the reintegration of meaning
and action does not, after all, depend on translating a particular
analysis into a corresponding strategy - which, in very different ways, represents both the liberal conception of problem-
solving and the Marxist conception of praxis - but of being
able to evoke from an analysis a sense of the relationships to be
created, a set of principles of action, broad enough to encourage and develop the kind of convergence I have discussed. The
changes which the older, richer, industrial capitalist societies
are undergoing constantly provoke issues where a choice is
being made between the two emerging paradigms I discussed
in the last chapter - questions of plant closures and the right
to a job; of developing new technologies for energy production,
communications, medicine, and who is to control them; questions
of the exploitation of resources, the dumping of waste, and the
accountability of firms; questions of arms production; of the
rights of women to control, equally with men, the circumstances
of their lives; and of people generally to take charge of managing the work they do, and of what happens to their neighbourhood. The outcome will depend on whether all those who oppose
the emerging international capitalist order can create an alliance
inclusive and ideologically open enough to give the alternative
paradigm the momentum of a realizable ideal.

7 CONCLUSION

The last of the Home Office Community Development Projects
ended in 1977. Some of the work they started still goes on,
struggling against bad housing and industrial decline. John
Benington and the Coventry Workshop are still working to
involve trade unions in community needs - but now under the
shadow of the near-bankruptcy of Coventry's motor industry.
The hope of rebuilding the Docklands' communities faded too.
In 1980, the Conservative government withdrew funding from
the Jubilee underground rail line, the last major project of the
once ambitious plans for Docklands' recovery, leaving only a
promise of a few road improvements, and a proposal for a 'free
enterprise zone', where new business would be attracted by
the minimum of taxation or regulation of any kind. In a weaken-
ing economy, under the policies of a rigid and unsympathetic
government, inner city communities could hope for very little
relief from economic and social decay. Even the social services
and grants in aid they had once been able to take for granted
were now under attack.

In the United States, too, fiscal conservatism, economic recession, a reaction of ruthlessness or indifference towards poverty
and social hardship left advocates and workers for inner city
communities with less political leverage and fewer resources
than at any time in the past twenty years. Yet the social and
economic problems they faced were greater than ever, and the
devastation more widespread. The energy for social change
tended inevitably to flow towards causes where there was more
hope of achievement - women's rights, the campaign against
nuclear power, environmental protection. A world where liberal
policies set the context for community struggles, ideological
debates and social analysis already seems old-fashioned. Looking back on the experience of community action, is there anything to be learned from that search for meaning and relevance
still useful to recall in a time of other issues and harsher ideologies?

To put the question in that way implies already one conclusion
from this history which I believe is very generally important
to the course of social movements. The ideological preoccupations which predominate in government greatly influence the
opportunities open even to its radical opponents, because that
ideology defines the moral and material expectations to which a
government commits itself, and which it cannot repudiate without putting its own legitimacy in question. The ability of

community action to attract resources and change policies
depended largely on the leverage these issues of legitimacy
afforded. President Johnson's commitment to eradicate poverty,
or the British Labour Party's commitment to egalitarian social
welfare, generated policies whose inauthenticity could be used
to hammer home the need for much better funded or more radical
means. The quality of the social ideals which inform policy discussions, political debates, journalism, television reporting,
and the attitudes of everyday life affect how movements for
change can challenge the legitimacy or performance of policy
and justify their own claims. It also affects the means which,
by virtue of the way an institution's legitimate functioning is
defined, must be open for reformers to use - the right to take
part in planning or policy, to apply for grants, publish evidence, or take legal action.

So long as government policy and community action justify
themselves by the same ideals, community action has scope for
influence on government's own terms, even if its ideology is in
other ways radically opposed to the assumptions of government.
But there is a risk that in attacking those assumptions, in
exposing how hypocritically or ineptly the ideals are being ful-
filled, and in defence against co-optation, the movement of
protest will undermine the sense that any shared framework
of ideals exists at all. It then has to justify itself entirely on
its own terms, creating its own moral consensus - and this
represents a task of organization and persuasion for which a
much broader base than deprived communities is needed. Movements of change are empowered, as the discussion of paradigms
suggested, by the convergence of social ideals expressed in
principles of action. To define these ideals in universal rather
than class terms does not pre-empt conflict but justifies it. So
the search to recover and define this shared sense of values,
to reformulate and continue a tradition of social idealism must
be part of any strategy of change. Otherwise, no movement can
exert more influence than the size and power of the interests
it represents.

The hardships characteristic of many inner city neighbourhoods - blighted surroundings, delapidated housing, unemployment, worse schools and services but greater need, all often
compounded by racial discrimination and the exploitation of
women's labour - are the hardships of a minority. Other workers,
in more prosperous suburbs, are more secure because of them;
other districts more whole. The Coventry team's analysis suggests how hard it would be to recruit a powerful coalition around
the needs of these impoverished inner city neighbourhoods, if
their struggle is interpreted purely as a class struggle.

In their final report, the Coventry Project explained the marginality of Hillfields as a cumulative burden of uncertainty,
passed down to them through a hierarchy of pre-emptive control.
At every level of government or economic organization, people
seek to displace the uncertainties of their situation on to others,

by holding open the widest possible range of actions for themselves while predetermining the response to whichever action
they choose. The measure of this control enables them to vary
their actions in unpredictable situations so that they still have
predictable consequences: and the greater the control, the more
likely that these consequences can be made to conform to their
purposes. Correspondingly, those with least control have the
narrowest range of adaptations open to them, and so the least
chance of being able to sustain the purposes which matter to
them. Their jobs, their community and their territory cannot
be protected against unpredictable variations in demand or
levels of support. They have no future that they can call their
own.

From this point of view, class conflict revolves around the
control of risks and the displacement of uncertainty on to others.
Everyone depends on some acknowledged bonds of mutual obli-
gation and support – between colleagues, workmates, family,
a congregation – to protect them against misfortune. This
community of mutual aid is the most fundamental form of social
insurance, underlying the creation and sustaining of institutionalized provisions. Solidarity is a crucial principle of survival.
But one aspect of this solidarity is collective defence against
any attempt by outsiders to increase their own protection at
your expense. The way in which people define the boundaries
of their community of mutual protection will, therefore, determine how they interpret the politics of risk. These boundaries
are themselves determined by the means of control over risks
which people share in common.

In the tradition of Marxist analysis, the ability to displace
the burden of uncertainty is assumed to rest in control over
the means of production; so there are essentially two classes,
owners and workers, between whom stands a cluster of self-
employed professionals, managers and small-business owners.
But in contemporary capitalist societies, with established trade
unions, closed shops, a very large sector of public employment
and jobs depending on public expenditures, where financial
security depends on a complex system of taxation and subsidy
unknown in Marx's day, the pragmatic pattern of protection
that binds one person to another in mutual defence cannot be
defined in simple terms of worker or capitalist. Home ownership, the right to decent local authority housing, rent control,
pension rights, the restrictive practices of professional associations, the maintenance of high levels of defence expenditure,
the regulation of interest rates, tax rebates, welfare rights
are all competing factors in how the burden of risk is distributed. They inevitably divide people according to a complex
and ambivalent sense of the boundaries of mutual solidarity. If
there is an overriding common interest underlying this competition – a fundamental alliance against capitalistic exploitation –
it is difficult to articulate, as an immediate concern, except
through these other institutions of mutual protection – as a

plea for solidarity with tenants seeking rent control, with women and men struggling against discrimination, with strikers or public employees struggling to save their jobs, with working families seeking tax cuts - where it becomes embroiled again in the conflicting consequences, for different kinds of workers and households, of each of these demands.

If the needs of inner city communities are to attract help, therefore, it is not enough to present them simply in classical terms of class exploitation, as if some emerging working-class consciousness will, of itself, sooner or later, come to grips with them. They also have to appeal to principles of social justice which society as a whole cannot ignore.

In terms of the analysis I have taken from the Coventry report, these issues of social justice involve the way the burden of uncertainty is distributed through the structure of social relationships. They must therefore also involve planning - since planning means, essentially, controlling uncertainty - either by taking action now to secure the future, or by preparing actions to be taken in case an event occurs. Both make the future more predictable and manageable in terms of present purposes.

The question, of course, is whose purposes? Planning for inner city communities has been discredited because it often increased the uncertainties for the people who lived there - displacing them carelessly, or leaving them in blighted, half-built and half-destroyed surroundings without knowing when or where they would move, while taking out more jobs, and more familiar and better paid jobs, than those it brought in. But to repudiate the idea of planning itself would be self-destructive. Without some collective strategy of action, able to control some events and adapt with foresight to others, there would be no way to distribute risks fairly. The Docklands Strategic Plan, for all its shortcomings, did try to set out a course of action which would take account of a wide range of community needs and purposes, and secure them against the inevitable uncertainties of the future as adaptively and fairly as possible. It evolved under constant pressure from the people of the dockside parishes, who had both a strong sense of their communities, and a long tradition of political action: and the professional advocates who helped them knew how to exploit the processes of planning - legal intervention, the gathering and analysis of data, the representation of community needs - to open issues to debate, so that this pressure could be productive.

The plan in the end had very little influence on the actual distribution of uncertainty and control. Because plans are so often ignored, whenever they attempt to set priorities and guarantees in the interests of the most vulnerable, or constrain the freedom of action of those more powerful so as to reach some resolution which is both fair and practicable, planning even at its best often comes to seem merely a distraction from more effective forms of political protest, and so co-optive. But the lesson of this is not to reject planning in favour of political

struggles, but to incorporate into those struggles a demand
for effective, open, collective planning, as a crucial part of
carrying out any practical ideal of social justice. Otherwise,
the struggle does not lead towards any resolution except competitive bargaining between different kinds of interests, and
that cannot protect the weaker and more vulnerable members
of society.

These three conclusions from the history of the Community
Development Project and the Docklands plan are, I think, relevant to any social action on behalf of the most disadvantaged:
that it needs a context of broadly shared ideals to which it can
appeal, and in whose terms it can challenge the legitimacy of
things as they are; that these ideals, as ideals of justice,
essentially involve the way the burden of uncertainty is distributed; and that planning is a necessary part of any process
of allocating this burden fairly. These principles apply to
reforms and more radical changes: the difference lies in whether
the ideals appealed to are represented as inherent in the present order of society or incompatible with it.

These conclusions have more to do with meanings than with
actions. From the point of view of many who worked in the Community Development Project, their experience suggested that
for the future, it would be better to work independently of
government, but more closely with organized workers, especially
on the shop floor, so as to draw together community issues of
housing, amenities and services with broader economic issues.
Once it has established its own base of organization and support, this alliance needs to include local government. Such a
combination of community organization, trade union organization
and local government could then begin to take back control of
the land, skills, revenue, assets, pension funds it collectively
owns to work out a co-operative plan for the social as well as
economic future. In the United States and Western Europe, new
conceptions of co-operative economic management are emerging,
directed towards security of employment and continuity of community rather than making the most of profits; although only a
few local authorities have begun to experiment with such radical
approaches in Britain.

But the reformulation of social meaning, redefining ideals
and principle, is perhaps needed now as much as any other
kind of action. The most advanced industrial societies are
undergoing a process of ideological disintegration, as the policies which sustained their prosperity falter and the rate of
economic growth declines. Few people still believe that the
disadvantaged will be swept up in an endless growth of wealth,
making poverty obsolete and inequality a trivial issue. The
idea of constant material progress itself begins to seem inherently self-destructive, overwhelming the adaptive capacity of
both the social and natural world. As people lose faith in an
ever-expanding economy, the contradictions between the egalitarian political ideals of democracy, and the reality of great

inequalities of wealth and entrenched racial disadvantages
become more harshly and cynically obtrusive.

Socialists have, I think, always tended to assume that when
this ideology of liberal capitalism collapsed - as they foresaw
that it must - most people would turn towards socialism, as
their true class interest became apparent to them. But in
practice, because the democratic socialist tradition shares so
many ideals in common with the liberalism it opposes - ideals
of liberty, tolerance, freedom of expression, social justice and
fundamental equality - it risks being discredited as only a more
extreme, and so even less convincing, version of the same
impractical humanism. So the ideologies which seem presently
to be gaining most power represent, in S.M. Miller's telling
phrase, a 'recapitalization of capital'[1] - a return to the ruthlessness of the nineteenth-century Poor Law reformers and classical economic doctrine, compounded by a crude, frightened,
diffuse impulse of self-protection at the expense of the weak.
At the same time, the disintegration of a broad, liberal consensus leaves politicians uncertain how to react to well-organized
and vocal advocates of repressive policies, who would deny
abortions, punish homosexuals, reinstate religious censorship,
expel black- or brown-skinned immigrants, or increase police
powers. These groups become dangerous because, irrespective
of their real numbers, the seriousness with which politicians
nervously treat them makes their ideas increasingly respected.
This combination of single issue fanaticism, self-protective
economic ruthlessness, and widespread ideological confusion
can lead to irrational but powerful alliances; and there is no
reassurance in history that the class interests of the majority
will come together to oppose them.

So it seems to me especially important now to draw feminism,
movements of racial equality, ecological and environmental
movements, together with liberal and socialist traditions to
reformulate and assert what the ideals of our societies should
be. Otherwise, the chance to create a broad, tolerant and
humane reintegration of meaning and action will be pre-empted.
If radicals have characteristically neglected this, it is perhaps
because their theoretical assumptions lead them to see ideologies only as the expression and rationalization of class interest - and so of little importance apart from the class conflict
they express. Ideals are pretty words, easily manipulated.
But the need for meaning is more profound and pervasive than
the need to rationalize. It structures life itself.

NOTES

1 Introduction
1 'Loss and Change', London, Routledge & Kegan Paul, 1974.
2 Karl Marx and Frederick Engels, 'The German Ideology', ed. and with Introduction by C.J. Arthur, New York, International Publishers, 1970, p. 64.
3 Ibid., p. 65.
4 Anthony Giddens, 'Central Problems in Social Theory: Action, Structure and Contradiction in Social Analysis', London, Macmillan, 1979, pp. 71-2.
5 Ibid., p. 72.

2 Community action
1 'Experiments in Social Policy and Their Evaluation, Report of an Anglo-American conference held at Ditchley Park, Oxfordshire, 29-31 October 1969', Community Development Project, Home Office, p. 1.
2 A.H. Halsey, Government against Poverty, paper presented to the Ditchley conference, p. 2. In the conference Report.
3 Ibid., p. 2.
4 Community Development Project - A General Outline, Home Office, mimeo, n.d.
5 Peter Marris and Martin Rein, 'Dilemmas of Social Reform', 1st edn, London, Routledge & Kegan Paul, 1967.
6 Ditchley conference Report, pp. 18-20.
7 Ibid., pp. 47-8.
8 John Greve, Research Strategy in C.D.P., Home Office, mimeo, n.d.
9 Community Development Project: Objectives and Strategies, Home Office, mimeo, 1970.
10 The twelve places were Canning Town and the Newington district of Southwark, in central London; Saltley in Birmingham; Hillfields in Coventry; Cleator Moor, Cumbria; Batley, Kirklees; Benwell in Newcastle-upon-Tyne; North Tyneside; Vauxhall in Liverpool; Oldham; Glyncorrwg, Glamorgan; Paisley, Scotland.
11 'Coventry CDP Final Report: Part 1: Coventry and Hillfields: Prosperity and the Persistence of Inequality', Home Office and City of Coventry in association with the Institute of Local Government Studies, March 1975, p. 6.
12 Ibid., p. 39.
13 Ibid., p. 37.
14 Ibid., p. 48.
15 National Community Development Project, Inter-Project Report to the Home Secretary, mimeo, n.d.
16 'The Costs of Industrial Change', London, CDP Inter-Project Editorial Team, January 1977.
17 Ibid., p. 96.
18 CDP, 'Gilding the Ghetto', London: Inter-Project Editorial Team, February 1977.
19 Alan Davis, Neil McIntosh and Jane Williams, 'The Management of Deprivation: Final Report of Southwark Community Development Project', London, Polytechnic of the South Bank, 1977, p. 50.

20   Ibid., p. 51.
21   Phil Topping and George Smith, 'Government Against Poverty? Liverpool
     Community Development Project, 1970-75', Oxford, Social Evaluation
     Unit, September 1977, p. 119.
22   Ibid., p. 15.
23   Ibid., p. 115.
24   Richard Penn and Jeremy Alden, 'Upper Afan CDP Final Report to
     Sponsors. Joint Report by Action Team and Research Team Directors',
     Cardiff, University of Wales, Institute of Science and Technology,
     July 1977.
25   'Gilding the Ghetto', p. 64.
26   Jan O'Malley, 'The Politics of Community Action', Nottingham, Bertrand
     Russell Peace Foundation for Spokesman Books, 1977, p. 32.
27   'Evening Standard', 9 May 1973, cited in O'Malley, op. cit., p. 137.
28   Ibid., pp. 164-5.
29   Ibid., p. 175.
30   'as a community project, we had no legitimacy in the eyes of the local
     Labour Movement - vis-à-vis industrial/economic issues. The legitimacy
     we had to win, by demonstrating our abilities to perform certain func-
     tions and offering certain facilities which could be used by Labour
     Movement bodies. But Labour Movement bodies are, quite rightly,
     suspicious of "outside" organizations which might be seen as interfering.'
     'North Shields: Living with Industrial Change', North Tyneside CDP,
     Final Report, vol. 2, Newcastle Polytechnic, 1978, p. 183.

3   *Planning in Docklands*

  1   Hugh Wilson and Lewis Womersley et al., 'Change or Decay. Final Report
      of the Liverpool Inner Area Study for the Department of the Environ-
      ment', London, HMSO, 1977; Graeme Shankland, Peter Willmott and
      David Jordan, 'Inner London: Policies for Dispersal and Balance. Final
      Report of the Lambeth Inner Area Study', London, HMSO, 1977;
      Llewelyn-Davies, Weeks, Forestier-Walker and Bor, 'Unequal City.
      Final Report of the Birmingham Inner Area Study', London, HMSO,
      1977; Department of the Environment, 'Inner Area Studies', summaries
      of consultants' final reports, London, HMSO, 1977.
  2   'Policy for the Inner Cities', cmnd 6845 London, HMSO, June 1977,
      pp. 2-3.
  3   Ibid., p. 3.
  4   Ibid., p. 5.
  5   Ibid., p. 1.
  6   John Pudney, 'London's Docks', London, Thames & Hudson, 1975.
  7   Ibid., p. 121, quoting H.L. Smith and Vaughan Nash, 'The Story of the
      Dockers' Strike 1889' (1889).
  8   Ibid., p. 155, quoting Francis Williams, 'Ernest Bevin', London,
      Hutchinson, 1952.
  9   Ibid., p. 177.
 10   Statement by Tower Hamlets Action Committee on Jobs, 1975.
 11   Detailed analyses of the decline in employment and industry in the five
      dockland boroughs are contained in 'Tower Hamlets: The Fight for a
      Future', Joint Docklands Action Group et al., December 1975; 'Work
      and Industry in East London', Docklands Joint Committee, April 1975;
      'Topic Paper on Employment', London Borough of Tower Hamlets,
      October 1976; 'Canning Town to North Woolwich: The Aims of Industry?',
      Canning Town CDP, January 1975; 'Employment in Southwark: A
      Strategy for the Future', Southwark Trades Council and Southwark
      CDP, May 1976.
 12   Repeated in a message in 'Turning Point', a pamphlet published by the
      Greater London Council, Autumn 1972.
 13   'Docklands Strategic Plan', Docklands Joint Committee, July 1976, p. 6.
 14   Travers Morgan, 'Dockland Study Report', London, 1973.
 15   Edward Johns, in an interview with the author.

16   Bringing the People into Planning, Report by the Leader of the GLC
     Docklands Team, Docks 7, Docklands Joint Committee, February 1974.
17   Report of the Officer's Steering Group on an Application by Action
     Groups for Urban Aid, Docks 23, Docklands Joint Committee, August
     1976.
18   'A Policy for Public Involvement in Docklands Development', Docklands
     Joint Committee, August 1974, p. 5. For the Joint Docklands Action
     Group's alternative proposals see 'Participation in the Planning of
     Docklands', Joint Dockland Action Group, 1 August 1974; and JDAG
     Discussion Paper on Membership of Advisory Group on Public Consulta-
     tion, October 1974, for their criticism of the official structure.
19   'Docklands Strategic Plan', p. 7.
20   Ibid., p. 32.
21   Ibid., p. 8.
22   Ibid., p. 23.
23   See 'Docklands: The Fight for the Future', Joint Docklands Action
     Group Resource Centre Discussion Paper, September 1977, for a general
     evaluation of the plan and its history as seen by the action groups'
     professional staff. A paper with the same title but published in April,
     1976, sets out the action groups' response to the plan's strategy.
24   David Eversley argues the case for a development corporation in 'The
     Redevelopment of London Docklands: A Case Study in Sub-Regional
     Planning', Regional Studies Association, Occasional Paper no. 1. which
     summarizes his evidence to the House of Commons Select Committee on
     Expenditure (Environment Sub-Committee) in February 1975. See also
     Peter Hall's response in 'New Society' (27 February 1975) to my article,
     Planning for People: The Docklands Example, published in 'New Society',
     the week before.
25   'Docklands Strategic Plan', p. 32.
26   Report by the Director of the Docklands Development Team on Proposed
     Trade Mart, Surrey Docks, Southwark, Docks 9, Docklands Joint
     Committee, 14 November 1974.
27   Interviews with Rod Robertson, Secretary of the Southwark Trades
     Council and Patrick Harris of the Southwark Docklands Action Group.
     Letters from Southwark Trades Council to Deputy Town Clerk, South-
     wark (16 August 1974) and to the Chairman, Docklands Joint Committee
     (16 June 1975).
28   Report by the Director of the Docklands Development Team on Trade
     Mart: Current Situation, Docks 57, Docklands Joint Committee, 24 March
     1975.
29   Joint statement issued by the Greater London Council and London
     Borough of Southwark, 5 November 1976.
30   Mr Flood, general manager of construction for the World Trade Centre,
     in an interview with the author.
31   'Conservation: A Guide to the Conservation Programme in the Redevelop-
     ment of the St Katherine's Docks, London', Taylor Woodrow Property
     Company, n.d.
32   Steve Haywood, Flower of the East? St Katharine's Present and Future,
     'Time Out', no. 392, 7-13 October 1977.
33   Report by the Director of the Dockland Development Team on The Sugar
     and Sugar Substitutes Industries in Docklands, Docks 199, Docklands
     Joint Committee, 9 June 1977. See also Nigel Moor, 'Jobs in Jeopardy'
     (A report to the National Community Development Project), June 1974,
     pp. 26-33.
34   Joint Docklands Action Group et al., 'Tower Hamlets: The Fight for a
     Future', pp. 19-22.
35   Nigel Moor, op. cit., pp. 20-6.
36   Greater London Council Press Release, Docklands: Dramatic Change
     for Better, 3 June 1977.
37   Report by the Director, Docklands Development Team on Government's
     Inner City Proposals: (i) White Paper, (ii) Construction Works,

Docks 201A, Docklands Joint Committee, 17 June 1977.
38 Joint Docklands Action Group Resource Centre, 'Docklands - The Fight for the Future' (Draft discussion paper, September 1977), p. 31.
39 Docklands Joint Committee, 'London Docklands Operational Programme 1978-82', Docks 282, July 1978, pp. 8-12. The plans for a new underground line were cancelled in July 1980.

4 *Employment, inflation and taxes*

1 Coventry Workshop, Progress Report 1976-77 Coventry Workshop, mimeo, January 1978, pp. 6-7.
2 The Institute of Workers' Control Committee of Enquiry into the Motor Industry, A Workers' Enquiry into the Motor Industry, Coventry, n.d.
3 Chrysler's Crisis: The Workers' Answer, submitted by a joint union delegation of shop stewards and staff representatives, 8 December 1975.
4 J.K. Galbraith, 'The New Industrial State', New York, New American Library, 1968, pp. 11-12.
5 'Daily Telegraph', 15 July 1976.
6 'A Workers' Enquiry into the Motor Industry', pp. 9-10.
7 'Chryslers' Crisis'.
8 See Anthony Sampson, 'The Seven Sisters', New York, Viking Press, 1975.
9 Robert Bacon and Walter Ellis, How We Went Wrong, 'Sunday Times', 2 November 1975.
10 Figures from US Bureau of the Census, 1950 and 1970, tabulated in Harvey S. Perloff, The Central City in the Post Industrial Age, in Charles L. Levin, ed., 'The Mature Metropolis', Lexington, Mass., Lexington Books, 1978.
11 Total expenditure of all levels of government in the United States rose from 12.8 per cent of GNP in 1945-50 to 22.4 per cent in 1966-70 (state and local government expenditure from 5.9 per cent to 11.5 per cent, national expenditure from 1.4 per cent plus 5.1 per cent to 2.4 per cent plus 8.5 per cent (non-military and defence). Education expenditures rose 57 per cent in 1955-60 and 80 per cent between 1965 and 1970. Income maintenance rose from 1.9 billion dollars of federal expenditure per annum average in 1960-5 to 6.5 billion dollars per annum average in 1967-9). Total government expenditure increased seventy-fold from beginning of century to 1960s.
In Britain public sector claims on Market output rose from about 120 million in 1962 to over 130 million in 1974. Share of industrial production going to non-industrial use rose from 58 per cent (1961) to 70 per cent (1974).
Local Government employment in the United States rose from 3,228,000 in 1950 to 7,102,000 in 1969; state government employment from 1,057,000 to 2,614,000. The increase was especially in education (25 per cent of state government employees in 1964, 40 per cent by 1966). Education workers expanded from 45 per cent to 55 per cent of local government employment between 1952 and 1966.
In Britain local government employment increased 53.8 per cent in 1961-73; Central government 14.4 per cent; non-government 7 per cent. Total growth in non-industrial employment in Britain 32 per cent. Educational employment increased more than any other, by 74 per cent (1961-73).
12 See, Theodore W. Schultz, Human Capital, 'International Encyclopedia of the Social Sciences', vol. II, New York, Macmillan and Free Press, 1968, pp. 278-87.
13 James O'Connor, 'The Fiscal Crisis of the State', New York: St. Martin's Press, 1973, for instance, presents public expenditure in this way, from a radical point of view.
14 Emergency Employment Act 1971, Title II.
15 William J. Baumol, Microeconomics of Unbalanced Growth: The Anatomy of the Urban Crisis, 'American Economic Review', June 1967.

16   John Dunlop, ed., 'The Theory of Wage Determination', London,
     Macmillan, 1957; see ch. 1, 'The Task of Contemporary Wage Theory'.
17   See Martin Rein and Peter Marris, Equality Inflation and Wage Control,
     'Challenge', March-April 1975.
18   For accounts of New York City's crisis see Roger E. Alcaly and David
     Mermelstein, eds, 'The Fiscal Crisis of American Cities: Essays on the
     Political Economy of Urban America with Special Reference to New York',
     New York, Vintage Books, 1977.
19   Jurgen Habermas, 'Legitimation Crisis', trans. Thomas McCarthy,
     Boston, Beacon Press, 1975, pp. 61-2.

5 *Paradigms*
   1   Thomas Kuhn, 'The Structure of Scientific Revolutions', 2nd edn,
       enlarged, University of Chicago Press, 1970.
   2   See, for instance, the essays by Stephen Toulmin and Margaret
       Masterman in Imre Lakatos and Alan Musgrave, eds, 'Criticism and
       the Growth of Knowledge', Cambridge University Press, 1970, which
       also includes Kuhn's reply.
   3   See, for instance, Richard M. Titmuss, 'Essays on the Welfare State',
       and 'Income Distribution and Social Change', London, Allen & Unwin,
       1958 and 1962; Brian Abel-Smith and Peter Townsend, 'The Poor and
       the Poorest', London, Bell, 1965; Bernard Frieden and Marshall
       Kaplan, 'The Politics of Neglect', Cambridge, Mass., MIT Press,
       1975; Peter Marris and Martin Rein, 'Dilemmas of Social Reform', London,
       Routledge & Kegan Paul, 1967.
   4   Frances Fox Piven, Whom Does the Advocate Planner Serve? in Richard
       A. Cloward and Frances Fox Piven, 'The Politics of Turmoil: Essays on
       Poverty, Race and the Urban Crisis', New York, Pantheon, 1974.
   5   S.M. Miller, The Recapitalization of Capital, 'Social Policy', September/
       October 1978.
   6   Richard J. Barnet and Ronald E. Miller, 'Global Reach: The Power
       of Multinational Corporations', New York, Simon & Schuster, 1974,
       p. 14.
   7   E.F. Schumacher, 'Small is Beautiful: Economics as if People Mattered',
       Introduction by Theodore Roszak, New York: Harper & Row, 1973;
       Ivan Illich, 'Medical Nemesis: The Expropriation of Health', New York,
       Pantheon, 1976; 'Tools for Conviviality', New York, Harper & Row,
       1973.
   8   See, for instance, Martin Carnoy and Derek Shearer, 'Economic Demo-
       cracy: The Challenge of the 1980s', New York, M.E. Sharpe, 1980.

6 *Metaphors*
   1   See, for instance, London-Edinburgh Weekend Return Group, 'In and
       Against the State', London, Publications Distributions Co-op, 1979.
       Several of the group had been involved with the Community Develop-
       ment Project.
   2   Harvey Sacks and Emmanuel Schegloff, A Simplest Systematics for the
       Organization of Turn-taking in Conversation, 'Language', vol. 50,
       1974.
   3   Erving Goffman, The Insanity of Place, in 'Frame Analysis', New York,
       Harper & Row, 1974.

BIBLIOGRAPHY

Individual authors

Abel-Smith, Brian, and Townsend, Peter, 'The Poor and the Poorest', London, Bell, 1965.

Alcaly, Roger E., and Memelstein, David, eds, 'The Fiscal Crisis of American Cities: Essays on the Political Economy of Urban America with Special Reference to New York', New York, Vintage Books, 1977.

Bacon, Robert, and Ellis, Walter, How We Went Wrong, 'Sunday Times', 2 November 1975.

Barnet, Richard J., and Miller, Roger E., 'Global Reach: The Power of Multinational Corporations', New York, Simon & Schuster, 1974.

Baumol, William J., Microeconomics of Unbalanced Growth: The Anatomy of the Urban Crisis, 'American Economic Review', June 1967.

Benington, John, Government Becomes Big Business, mimeo.

Carnoy, Martin, and Shearer, Derek, 'Economic Democracy: The Challenge of the 1980s', New York, M.E. Sharpe, 1980.

Dunlop, John, ed., 'The Theory of Wage Determination', London, Macmillan, 1957.

Eversley, David, The Redevelopment of London Docklands: A Case Study in Sub-Regional Planning, Regional Studies Association, Occasional Paper no. 1, 1975.

Frieden, Bernard, and Kaplan, Marshall, 'The Politics of Neglect', Cambridge, Mass., MIT Press, 1975.

Galbraith, John Kenneth, 'The New Industrial State', New York, New American Library, 1968.

Giddens, Anthony, 'Central Problems in Social Theory: Action, Structure and Contradiction in Social Analysis', London, Macmillan 1979.

Goffman, Erving, The Insanity of Place, in 'Frame Analysis', New York, Harper & Row, 1974.

Greve, John, Research Strategy in C.D.P., Home Office, mimeo, n.d.

Habermas, Jurgen, 'Legitimation Crisis', trans. Thomas McCarthy, Boston, Beacon Press, 1975.

Halsey, A.H., Government Against Poverty, in 'Experiments in Social Policy and Their Evaluation', Ditchley Conference Report, Home Office, 1969.

Haywood, Steve, Flower of the East? St Katharine's Present and Future, 'Time Out', no. 392, 7-13 October 1977.

Illich, Ivan, 'Tools for Conviviality', New York, Harper & Row, 1973.

— 'Medical Nemesis: The Expropriation of Health', New York, Pantheon, 1976.

Kuhn, Thomas, 'The Structure of Scientific Revelutions', 2nd edn, enlarged, University of Chicago Press, 1970.

Lakatos, Imre, and Musgrave, Alan, eds, 'Criticism and the Growth of Knowledge', Cambridge University Press, 1970.

Llewelyn-Davies, Weeks, Forestier-Walker and Bor, 'Unequal City, Final Report of the Birmingham Inner Area Study', London, HMSO, 1977.

London-Edinburgh Weekend Return Group, 'In and Against the State', London, Publications Distribution Co-op, 1979.

Marris, Peter, 'Loss and Change', London, Routledge & Kegan Paul, 1974.

— Planning for People: The Docklands Example, 'New Society', 27 February 1975.

Marris, Peter, and Rein, Martin, 'Dilemmas of Social Reform', 1st edn,

London, Routledge & Kegan Paul, 1967.
Marx, Karl, and Engels, Frederick, 'The German Ideology', ed. and with an
  Introduction by C.J. Arthur, New York, International Publishers, 1970.
Miller, S.M., The Recapitalization of Capital, 'Social Policy', September/
  October 1978.
Moor, Nigel, 'Jobs in Jeopardy: A Study of Job Prospects in Older Industrial
  Areas', Report to the National Community Development Project, June 1974.
O'Connor, James, 'The Fiscal Crisis of the State', New York, St. Martin's
  Press, 1973.
O'Malley, Jan, 'The Politics of Community Action', Nottingham, Bertrand
  Russell Peace Foundation for Spokesmen Books, 1977.
Perloff, Harvey S., The Central City in the Post Industrial Age, in Charles
  L. Levin, ed., 'The Mature Metropolis', Lexington Books, 1978.
Piven, Frances Fox, Whom Does the Advocate Planner Serve? in Richard A.
  Cloward and Frances Fox Piven, 'The Politics of Turmoil: Essays on Poverty,
  Race and the Urban Crisis', New York, Pantheon, 1974.
Pudney, John, 'London's Docks', London, Thames & Hudson, 1975.
Rein, Martin, and Marris, Peter, Equality, Inflation and Wage Control,
  'Challenge', March-April 1975.
Sacks, Harvey, and Schegloff, Emmanuel, A Simplest Systematics for the
  Organization of Turn-Taking in Conversation, 'Language', vol. 50, 1974.
Sampson, Anthony, 'The Seven Sisters', New York, Viking Press, 1975.
Schultz, Theodore W., Human Capital, 'International Encyclopedia of the
  Social Sciences', vol. II, New York, Macmillan and Free Press, 1968.
Schumacher, E.F., 'Small is beautiful: Economics as if People Mattered',
  New York, Harper & Row, 1973.
Shankland, Graeme, Willmott, Peter and Jordan, David, 'Inner London:
  Policies for Dispersal and Balance. Final Report of the Lambeth Inner Area
  Study', London, HMSO, 1977.
Taylor Woodrow Properties Company, 'Conservation: A Guide to the Con-
  servation Programme in the Redevelopment of the St Katharine's Docks',
  London, n.d.
Titmuss, Richard M., 'Essays on the Welfare State', London, Allen & Unwin,
  1958.
—'Income Distribution and Social Changes', London, Allen & Unwin, 1962.
Travers Morgan, 'Dockland Study Report', London, 1973.
Wilson, Hugh, and Womersley, Lewis, et al., 'Change on Decay. Final Report
  of the Liverpool Inner Area Study for the Department of the Environment',
  London, HMSO, 1977.

Community Development Project reports and publications
'Experiments in Social Policy and Their Evaluation, Report of an Anglo-
  American conference held at Ditchley Park, Oxfordshire, 29-31 October
  1969', Community Development Project, Home Office.
'Community Development Project - A General Outline', Home Office, mimeo, n.d.
'Community Development Project: Objectives and Strategies', Home Office,
  mimeo, 1970.
'Canning Town, to North Woolwich: The Aims of Industry?', (Canning Town
  CDP, January, 1975).
'Coventry CDP Final Report: Part I, Coventry and Hillfields: Prosperity and
  the Persistence of Inequality', Home Office and City of Coventry in associa-
  tion with the Institute of Local Government Studies, March 1975.
'Employment in Southwark: A Strategy for the Future', Southwark Trades
  Council and Southwark CDP, May 1976.
Inter-Project Report to the Home Secretary, National Community Development
  Project, mimeo, n.d.
'The Costs of Industrial Change', London, CDP Inter-Project Editorial Team,
  January 1977.
'Gilding the Ghetto', London, CDP Inter-Project Editorial Team, February
  1977.
'The Management of Deprivation: Final Report of Southwark Community

Development Project', Alan Davis, Neil McIntosh, Jane Williams, London, Polytechnic of the South Bank, 1977.

'Upper Afan CDP Final Report to Sponsors. Joint Report by Action Team and Research Team Directors', Richard Penn and Jeremy Alden, Cardiff, University of Wales, Institute of Science and Technology, July 1977.

'Government Against Poverty? Liverpool Community Development Project 1970-75', Phil Topping and George Smith, Oxford, Social Evaluation Unit, September 1977.

'North Shields: Living with Industrial Change', North Tyneside CDP, Final Report, vol. 2, Newcastle Polytechnic, 1978.

National British government papers

Department of the Environment, 'Inner Area Studies', summaries of consultants' final reports, London, HMSO, 1977.

'Policy for the Inner Cities', cmnd 6845, London, HMSO, June 1977.

Local government papers

London Borough of Tower Hamlets, 'Topic Paper on Employment', October 1976.

Greater London Council, 'Turning Points', (Autumn, 1972).

Joint Docklands Action Group papers

'Participation in the Planning of Docklands', 1 August 1974.

J.D.A.G. Discussion Paper of Membership of Advisory Group on Public Consultation, October 1974.

'Tower Hamlets: The Fight for a Future', December 1975.

Tower Hamlets Action Committee, 'Statement on Jobs', mimeo, 1975.

'Docklands: The Fight for the Future', Joint Docklands Action Group Resource Centre Discussion Paper, September 1977.

'Rebuilding Docklands: Cuts and the Need for Public Investment', September 1977.

Docklands Joint Committee papers

'A Policy for Public Involvement in Docklands Development', August 1974.

'Work and Industry in East London', April 1975.

'Docklands Strategic Plan', July 1976.

'London Docklands Operational Programme 1978-82', Docks 282, July 1978.

Reports by the Director, Docklands Development Team

Bringing the People into Planning, Docks 7, February 1974.

Proposed Trade Mart, Surrey Docks, Southwark, Docks 9, 14 November 1974.

Report of the Officers' Steering Group on an Application by Action Groups for Urban Aid, Docks 23, August 1976.

Trade Mart: Current Situation, Docks 57, 24 March 1975.

The Sugar and Sugar Substitutes Industries in Docklands, Docks 199, 9 June 1977.

Government's Inner City Proposals: (i) White Paper (ii) Construction Works, Docks 201A, 17 June 1977.

Coventry Workshop papers

Progress Report 1976-77, Coventry, mimeo, January 1978.

The Institute of Workers' Control Committee of Enquiry into the Motor Industry, A Worker's Enquiry into the Motor Industry, Coventry, n.d.

Chrysler's Crisis: The Workers' Answer, submitted by a joint union delegation of shop stewards and shift representatives, 8 December 1975.

INDEX

Abel Smith, Brian, 98
action groups, Docklands, see
   Docklands Action Groups
administrators, role of, 18, 21
Advisory Council on Docklands
   Planning, 55
advocacy planning, 99–100
anti-poverty programmes in US, 11,
   16, 86, 87; see also Community
   action; United States
auctions, disrupted, 37–8

Batley Community Development Project,
   36
Benington, John, 23–4, 25, 26, 30, 41,
   45, 73, 75, 81, 103, 123
Bevin, Ernest, 48
boundaries, effect on planning, 59
Brawne, Rhoda, 57
British Leyland Motor Corporation, 73,
   76

Campaign for Economic Democracy,
   108
Canning Town Community Development
   Project, 55
capital, recapitalization of, 103
capitalism: class structure, 125–6;
   and conformity, 114; and loss of
   class solidarity, 105; Marxist
   analysis of, 7; as structure, 111
Centre for Environmental Studies, 30
Children's Department, Home Office, 13
Chrysler Corporation, 74, 75
Civil Rights Movement, 118, 119
class: and ideology, 7; and radical
   organizations, 91–2; and structure,
   112; uncertainty displaced by, 125–6;
   see also, working class
clothing industry, 66–7
Common Market, 66
Communist Manifesto, 103
Community Action: American experience of, 11–12; British and
   American contrasts in, 17; fallacies
   of, 15; in Notting Hill, 37–8; see
   also anti-poverty programmes
Community Development Project: and
   advocacy, 99; aftermath of, 123;

areas chosen for, 21–2, 129;
   compared to Docklands, 69; compared to Notting Hill, 38, 40;
   conclusions of, 32–3, 127; consensus
   of ideals in, 71; dilemma of co-
   optation or marginality in, 110;
   and distribution of uncertainty, 58;
   Ditchley conference on, 11; Home
   Office conception of, 14–15, 17; as
   illustrative case, 2, 100; initial
   assumptions underlying, 20–1, 43;
   Inter-Project Report of, 30; origins
   of, 13; policy conception undermined, 87; professional dilemmas of,
   32–6; qualities of professional staff,
   72; research in, 19, 20, 21;
   structural analysis by, 111
community organizers, as intellectual
   mediators, 3
conformity, 113–14, 116–18
conversational rules, 113
Cooper, Joan, 13
corporate management, 27
corporations, growth of, 97–8; multi-
   national, 104, 105; policy paradigm
   favoured by, 102; power of, 89
Coventry City, 22–3, 75
Coventry Community Development
   Project, 23, 24–6, 34, 73, 124, 126;
   final report of, 26, 27–8, 33, 45;
   see also Benington, John
Coventry Corporation, 25, 26–7, 103
Coventry Workshop, 73, 76, 108, 123
Cutler, Horace, 67

defence expenditure, 77
developers, and planning, 52, 65
Ditchley Park, 11; conference at,
   11–18, 20, 40, 71
Dockers' Strike of 1889, 47–8
Docklands: boundaries of, 46, 50, 51,
   55, 59; as case history, 2, 100;
   Conservative policies towards, 100;
   and control of uncertainty, 58;
   decline of manufacturing employment
   in, 66; employment in, 49; first
   attempt to plan, 53–5, 61; free
   enterprize zones in, 103; Government
   expenditures in, 67–8; industrial